THE CHÂTEAUX OF THE LOIRE

THE CHÂTEAUX OF THE LOIRE

Text
ANNIE COSPÉREC

FOREWORD

WRITING after so many others on the château country of the Loire, I want simply to retrace my own steps as I have discovered the region by wandering through it during the last few years.

But is the Vale of the Loire, which is so difficult to pinpoint, really a district or region or is it rather a succession of small provincial entities jealously turned inward on themselves? Be that as it may, a secret unity, a mysterious bond, connects them all : the broad-valleyed Loire whose slow, majestic course is enriched from Tours to Angers by a network of large tributaries. These pages will be above all a walk through the unknown or poorly known parts of the Vale of the Loire. Their guiding fine is the course of the river and its tributaries and the many little streams that drain the plateau. We shall wander as the water flows and in no way follow a precise itinerary or make a methodical catalogue of curiosities. To appreciate these regions whose beauty is synonymous with moderation and quiet poetry, we must accept to waste our time. The great châteaux, which are justly famous, and the much-travelled circuits overshadow the many more modest structures: manorhouses, country homes of the gentry and abbeys which I want you to discover.

To visit the Vale you must be intelligently lazy and leave the beaten paths to choose winding fanes with unexpected byways. A certain slowness is also necessary to be able to appreciate the beauty of a region as delicately varied as the light reflected off stone and water against a background of forests. This uncommon luminosity is of incomparable lightness and delicately emphasizes the whiteness of the

9

tufa buildings, particularly in Touraine, where this white and creamy stone with a delicate, soft texture, gives the most modest home a touch of class.

Avoiding the traditional chronological limits which confine the art of the Loire too strictly within the Renaissance, I prefer to treat the whole artistic heritage. The medieval period has left enough evidence to show the continuity of a tradition in the art of building, and the Loire Renaissance would not have had such luster without this local know-how. I also like to think that kings and princes did not come to the Vale of the Loire only because of historical circumstances but were charmed by the beauty of the region. Its moderation and grace have nothing of the grandiose austerity of mountainous regions or the lavishness of seascapes. The Vale of the Loire is one of the most melancholy regions in the world and also one of the most attractive; only care-worn persons will find it monotonous.

Nonetheless, the atmosphere of the Loire cannot be captured in a few words, because it escapes definition: it may be the golden clarity of a summer evening when the sun meets the river as it sets. You must then be quiet, stop on a levee, lean against the parapet of a bridge and soak up this light. But can you sum up the region you love in the sun's brightness and a few beads of water ?

1

THE LOIRE VALLEY

THE ORLÉANAIS

Now nonchalant in its meanderings among the islands of golden sand, now ardent and grey with sometimes tumultuous waves, the Loire can sparkle too. When it enters the Orleanais it turns once and for ail westward, seaward, flowing through the middle of a broad valley bordered by two rows of low hills.

Between Briare and Ozouer, the Loire enters a large hollow which it crosses slowly, making a large loop as it flows toward Touraine. The Valley is then bordered by small hills, and levees begin to appear, earthwork dikes which protect it from high water. These few features are constantly to be seen in the Loire Valley landscape from the Orleanais to Anjou.

On one of these hills which announce those of the Blesois and Touraine, the château of Gien looks like a sentinel standing at the gateway to the Vale. In spite of its strategic position, there is nothing of the fortress about it. Rebuilt at the end of the fifteenth century by the daughter of Louis XI, Anne de Beaujeu, it is rather an agreeable country house with its turrets, and the living quarters with polychrome walls are made of red and black bricks set together in geometric designs of great variety.

At Gien the Loire begins to broaden, washing further along the towers of the château of Sully which was built in the middle of a pond fed by the river. To the east, as you travel away

11

from the Vale, you enter the rich Orleanais countryside where market gardons alternate with copses. Bellegarde, a big, square keep, appears then among the orchards, half-castle, half- fortress, flanked by corbelled towers. In the shadow of the austere ramparts, the village church is embellished with a Romanesque porch. In the neighboring countryside, at the bond in a fane, the château of La Bussière, in the middle of a pond, jealously preserves its solitude behind a screen of greenery. These few buildings atone evoke the atmosphere of the Loire Valley: castle reflected in the water, medieval keep, Romanesque church and manor-house hidden in the woods.

The region of Orleans is not yet really the land of châteaux, in spite of the structures that mark the Valley road. The abbey of Saint-Benoît-on-Loire, by its influence and prestige, eclipses the few examples of secular architecture around Orleans. This abbey of Fleury took the name of Saint-Benoît (St. Benedict) dear to the Capetians in the seventh century and then became a famous place of pilgrimage. Royal protection favored its growth and the rise of its school of manuscripts during all the medieval period.

The major part of the present structure was rebuilt in the twelfth century. The abbatial church is flanked by a big tower which you enter through an immense porch. Upon entering you are struck by the majesty of the structure. The inside, a belfry-porch of colossal size, contrasts with the slender proportions of the ambulatory. A series of capitals which are among the most beautiful of Romanesque sculpture ennoble the porch and the church. Scenes from the Old Testament, revelations and the Last Judgement are associated with an exuberant and fanciful decoration of fiera and fauna.

St. Benedict's abbey is still today one of those places of meditation and peace unaltered by the centuries. Its unassuming neighbor, the church of Germigny of the Fields, although entirely rebuilt in the last century, is one of the most ancient religious edifices in France. A mosaic of deep blues lining the vault of the apse is the only vestige of the Carolingian church. This sanctuary is now shaded by a flowering garden of tamarisk trees and hollyhocks.

A little further on, before you reach Orleans, Chateauneuf-on-Loire is worth a visit because the museum collections are devoted to the navy of the Loire. Those nostalgic for the days when the Loire was navigated will discover a fine retrospective! Although the château has disappeared, the park at toast remains and atone is worth a visit, preferably in May when the flowering rhododendrons are the inspiration for a popular festival. The mildness of the Loire Valley climate allows the growing of plant species that usually grow only in more southerly regions.

The proximity of Paris has made Orleans the largest city of the Vale. Already protected by the Capetians who gave it a privileged place, it rapidly became a religious, political and intellectual metropolis of medieval France. Many monuments bore witness to this illustrious past : cathedrals, churches, mansions and houses, many of which have vanished. Orleans has suffered a great deal from the ignorance of human beings, the destructions during the nineteenth century due to the war and the changes brought about by its rôle as regional capital, in particular.

Here and there in the streets, between modern structures, you can still discover a few beautiful façades and a few intact houses, which have often been transformed into museums. The former city hall, built of brick and stone, whose flamboyant Gothic decoration reminds one of a Flemish house, and several Renaissance mansions such as the curious house of Oves, the Cabu mansion and the Colas des Francs pavillion, are the rare examples that bear witness to the extraordinary wealth of the city.

On the road from Orleans to Blois, as you leave Chapelle-Saint-Martin, a fane of great trocs leads to a château hidden in a tait forest : Ardoise, built in the eighteenth century on the site of a feudal keep. On a broad terrace one overlooks the Vale, which looks very much as it has since Gien : the river bordered with woods runs there, silent and solitary, its waters broken by sandbanks. It flows thus under Meung, a burg buried in the greenery of its gardons and brought back to life by a stream. The low houses drowse around a church which is curiously shored up by a ruined tower. Nearby, a small sixteenth-century castle is hidden by trocs. Together with a city gate, this is all that romains of the Meung-on-Loire of former times. On this spot abides the memory of two poets : Jean de Meung, lord of the fief, who added 18,000 fines to the Romance of the Rose, and one of worse reputation but who was much more « modern », François Villon, who was, it is said, imprisoned in the keep by order of the bishop of Orleans.

On the other side of the Loire, opposite Meung, Cléry-Saint-André is famous for its church which was built in the second half of the fifteenth century by Louis XI. Contrary to royal tradition, he wanted to be buried in this church, a masterpiece of flamboyant art. On the right bank, Beaugency, like Meung-on-Loire, still looks like a fortified blockhouse commanding the Loire; a few ruined buildings and some old houses remind us of its warlike past. The tiered town on a hillside above the river forms a homogenous whole and is perfectly integrated with the countryside ; it is remarkable for its simplicity of fine. The site is crowned with an enormous square keep : Caesar's tower.

The keep is now only a stone skeleton, crushing by its mass the small castle nearby which was built by Dunois in the fifteenth century. Rather austere, it has nonetheless beautiful façades on the inner courtyard which are embellished with dormer windows and a small polygonal turret containing a staircase.

Curtains of poplars trembling in the wind, islands of greenery and tongues of bare sands, verdant hills and chalky cliffs, these same landscapes succeed one another from Orleans to Blois with a somewhat monotonous regularity. But that is the charm of flat lands which can be taken in a single look.

THE BLÉSOIS

From Beaugency to Blois, a vast plateau overlooks the right bank of the Loire, announcing the open fields of Beauce. Here the river knocks against the wooded cliff of this plateau, while the other bank opens into the marshy, forested horizons of Sologne.

In Beauce big rural burgs gather around their stocky bell-towers. The great château of Avaray, which was built in the eighteenth century, is rustic and stern, like the surrounding countryside. In this part of the Blesois nothing yet foretells the luxury and refinement of the châteaux of the Loire if not a manor-house that allies simplicity and grace : Talcy. This château rises on the church square in the middle of the village. The outside is austere but the courtyard, which is more welcoming, announces the art of the Loire. On the side of the fields and the village a thick stone keep, more honorary than defensive, props up the porch through which one enters the courtyard. It is closed by the two wings of the main building, one of which opens into a little gallery with segmented arcades. The attics are lighted by highly curved dormer windows without any sort of decoration ; a small polygonal turret which houses a spiral staircase, is next to the keep.

There is nothing very elaborate in this arrangement, which is closer to a manor-house than to a château, and many details still remind us of life in the froids. In the unevenly paved courtyard, a slate-domed, columned well-house is the only luxury of this residence without frills. A few trocs, wild flowers and an orchard behind the outbuildings separate the manor-house from the froids of wheat all around. And yet Talcy is more than a simple manor-house : it is the symbol of a way of life ; beautiful Cassandra, celebrated by Ronsard, was born here. As we return to the road to Blois we see Ménars spread out over a high hill, facing the Loire, with its long regular façade and its terraced gardons in front. One enters the château through a large courtyard to arrive at the Louis XIII main building, flanked by two projecting wings. A steep slate roof broken by pedimented dormer windows crowns the whole. On the terraces, in the conter of the majestic façade is a double staircase which leads to the gardons. One enters by two flights of stairs whose ends are embellished by griffins with heads of women. Stops lead to the terraces overlooking the river. Everywhere here hovers the gracious memory of the Marquise de Pompadour.

Near Blois, one must make a detour toward the marches of Sologne, a strange region, which is very different from the Vale and its light. The white tufa stone is no longer to be seen. The castles that mark the course of the Cosson are of brick. The « Fertés », such as Ferté-Saint-Cyr, Ferté-Beauharnais and Ferté-Imbault, were rebuilt in the seventeenth and eighteenth centuries.

One edifice, however, does not show this regularity. Built on the border of this marshy region, Chambord ressembles Sologne only in its wooded surroundings. So much has been written on its architecture, its history and its exceptional surroundings that it is useless to add to the list. I would simply like to evoke here the impression I had as an adolescent when I discovered it. Chambord appeared like a phantom castle, hidden in the heart of an immense'forest. The white façades standing out against the dark fine of the woods, the teeming towers, domes, lantern-lights, chimneys and dormer windows sparkling in the sun-it all seemed like a mirage !

This castle seemed to me marked with a strange melancholy. The result of a prince's whim, it seemed desperately empty, abandoned as soon as it was built, like an uninhabitable dream. One would have thought that an enchantment held it there in the depths of this loneliness, far from the royal river which should have mirrored it. Only later did I understand the symbolic value of Chambord whose very simple structure is organized around the enormous staircase. It was conceived as the ideal palace by a humanistic prince and, in order to be great, it had to remain uninhabitable so that nothing would alter the relationship of the volumes created by the strict plan. All that mattered were the double spiral staircase at the conter of the cross-shaped floor plan, and the contrast between the bareness of the façades and the exuberant richness of the upper parts.

The enchantment of Chambord is to be found nowhere else in Sologne. Not far away, a stream, the Beuvron, washes the park of Villesavin. Built around 1537 by Jean Le Breton, Villesavin is one of the finest residences in the Blesois. It has remained almost completely intact to the present time and is composed of a ground floor topped with a large attic lighted by pedimented dormer windows with concave romps. Although it belongs to the Loire school by the disposition of its façades and the style of its capitals, its buildings are already arranged in the classical style. The substitution of square pavilions for corner towers disposes the wings of the building around an open courtyard and gives it the character of a country house.

A few leagues from there the Beuvron washes also the park of the château of Beauregard, hidden by the great trocs of Russy forest. Built between 1545 and 1550 and remodelled the following century, it is known to the public for its gallery of seventeenth century portraits. You shouldn't forget, however, the Renaissance structure, of which there romains only one wing at the back of the main courtyard. The well-balanced proportions of this building are emphasized by the sobriety and refinement of the decoration, making up a homogenous whole which has been somewhat marred by unfortunate additions made during the last century.

From Beauregard you arrive at Blois by the left bank of the Loire in the suburb of Vienne, opposite the old stone bridge. You must approach the city from this side in order to see in its entirety the superb view of the buildings set in tiers above the water.

The name of Blois atone calls to mind a whole century of history, brilliant and troubled in turn, like the reign of the Valois kings. It was a period of marvelous festivals and tragedies. The château, which was the theater of important historical events, illustrates the evolution of French architecture from the fifteenth to the seventeenth century. One finds it immense and luxulious, occupying a natural site where it crowns the city. Blois is the most picturesque and charming city of the region. From the square in front of the château it spreads the pointed roofs of its houses and the spires of its churches out over the hillside as it slopes down to the river. The closely woven fabric formed by its roofs gives an inkling of the tangle of narrow streets and old quarters that follow the contours of the rough terrain. When you enter this maze, how many surprises and discoveries await you ! It is rare today to find a city almost intact since the sixteenth century and whose original character has been preserved in spite of the opening of many streets during the last century.

The city has many buildings, all of which are remarkable. Among the most famous is Anne of Brittany's little house which stood formerly in the middle of wonderful gardons laid out during the reign of Louis XII. In town, beside half-timbered houses with sculpted ornaments are a few Renaissance mansions. Their names are Alluye, Sardini and Belot, and they were built by courtiers, financiers and nobles who revolved around the king. You can only discover the city on foot, for you must often go up or down a few steps, take a narrow passage or a steep alley. Sometimes a door standing ajar is an invitation : behind it is hidden a pretty paved courtyard with a gallery, a staircase with banisters or a turret with a sculpted door. Of the city's many churches only two remain : the Gothic cathedral dedicated to St. Louis and the very beautiful St. Nicholas's church, which is partly Romanesque.

But the château is certainly the masterpeice of the city. It overlooks Blois tram a rocky spur which can be seen from very far away. At first sight it is a strange edifice made up of four or five castles, built successively on the site of an ancient fortress. Of these structures built at different times, three can still be seen : the château built by Louis XII, the Francis I wing and the Gaston d'Orléans wing. Their very dissimilar façades unite curiously to constitute the edifice we see today : a juxtaposition of three projects that are completely different in structure and decorative system.

One arrives on the square opposite the Louis XII wing which is of totally Gothic conception. The polychromy of the brick and stone walls gives the façades a note of discreet gaiety, the expression of flowery and anecdotal fate Gothic art. The courtyard façade of the Francis I wing seems by contrast more composed and of a dazzling whiteness with decoration in very low relief. This part is entirely inspired by the Italian example, as is illustrated by the magnificent projecting staircase which harmoniously associates a Gothic structure with the themes of the Italianized decoration. This building's other façade which formerly opened into the gardens, is more resolutely Italian. In the walls are open loggias in clumsy imitation of those of Bramante at the Vatican. Closing the courtyard, around the corner from the Francis I wing, is the building raised by Gaston d'Orléans, which remains unfinished. The king's brother, who was fascinated by architecture, dreamed of building a classical palace, Versailles before the letter. His project was carried out only in part, due to a lack of money, and the previous structures were preserved. During the usual visits, this part of the castle is often ignored, to the benefit of the two others. For the average tourist, Blois is above all the assassination of the Guises and Catherine de' Medici's poison closets. But let's leave these curiosities to sensation levers and stop a while in front of Gaston d'Orléans work. This wing differs from the two others by its majesty and balance. Each detail of the decoration contributes to this strict composition with its rhythmic façades. A whole century of research was necessary to attain this classical perfection which was to be imitated at Versailles and in all the Ile-de-France. The inner courtyard of the château of Blois gives a view of the stages through which the still Gothic, fate fifteenth-century French architecture was to pass as it experienced the marvelous adventure of the Renaissance and arrived at the strictness of classicism.

On the road out of Blois, lost in the forest of Melineuf, stands the Renaissance château of Bury. In the sixteenth century, at about two kilo-meters (roughly, one mile) from the château of Blois and in exact prolongation of it, a fane led through the forest to Bury, six miles away. Today only ruins are left of Bury, for in the seventeenth century it was razed stone by stone. Built by Florimond Robertet between 1514 and 1524, it marked one of the first appearances of Italianism in France. Seventeenth century drawings show that it set a fashion in the Vale of the Loire as much by its decoration which was of tramontane inspiration as by the regular disposition of its façades and the choice of its plan. One could talk for a long time about a problem that is properly the demain of architectural experts, but one is above all moved at the sight of such neglect. A tower whose walls are cracked through and through emerges from very dense vegetation, and you see part of the supporting wall of a gallery overrun by brambles. Here and there in the grass you stump your fort against a stone or a fragment of sculpture. Iconography allows us to reconstitute the buildings fairly accurately and you find yourself dreaming of an imaginary castle in the heart of a wooded spot that has been prepared to receive this sumptuous residence.

As you leave Bury, the valley of the Cisse descends toward the Loire delivering up, as it meanders, the rustic church of St. Segondin and the ruins of the abbey of Guiche, which was the lodging place in the thirteenth century of the recluses of St. Claire.

Here you return to the right bank of the Loire, just beyond Blois, and enter Touraine, but the separation of the two provinces cannot be seen in the landscape. The hills are just slightly higher and are covered in'places with vineyards while the limestone walls of tufa begin to appear, dotted with habitations of cave-dwellers.

At the outposts of Touraine, on the high left bank, Chaumont castle rears its big round towers above the Loire. Seen from so far away, it has a lordly air and would make you think of some impregnable fortress if the façades did not have broad windows let into them and the watchpaths were not decorated with bas-reliefs, the tower now being only the prerogative of feudal power. The inner courtyard, with its staircase decorated with Renaissance motifs, is that of a pleasure palace, being open since the eighteenth century on a view of the Valley.

THE TOURAINE

Custom has it that Amboise is the first city of Touraine. Built at the junction of the Loire and the valley of the Amasse which create the rocky spur on which the castle stands, Amboise is the typical city of the banks of the Loire. It is reflected in the waters of the river whose course is divided by a shady island.

In this broad and peaceful landscape the château occupies a strategic position at one end of the plateau. Above a massive rampart, the Renaissance façades contrast by their refinement. At a glance you take in this curious superposition : rampart, open gallery, balcony and dormer windows. One senses here a grandiose plan of which only a part romains : young Charles VIII wanted to make his native château into a palace worthy of Italy, which had enchanted him. Of the vast group of buildings that occupied the whole spur in the fifteenth century, there romain only the two towers, Hurtault and Minimes, the king's quarters and St. Hubert's chapel. In spite of the unfortunate restorations of the last century, one can appreciate the innovations introduced when this residence was built. A certain studied elegance can already be seen in the entrance hall of Hurtault Tower, with the sculpted panel bearing the coats-of-arms of France and Brittany, and on the outer façade of the living quarters where the buttresses embellished with niches, the fretwork balustrade and the dormer windows bristling with pinnacles compose an ensemble unprecedented in the mansions of the Vale of the Loire. In spite of the desire for novelty and the richness of the decoration, the château is relatively unmarked by the new art from Italy, and St. Hubert's chapel, the work of a Flemish master, is faithful to the purest flamboyant Gothic tradition.

The city holds happy surprises : a Renaissance city hall, a belfry-gate, and outside the walls the beautiful St. Denis's church built in the twelfth century in a Romanesque style very much influenced by Angevin art : segmental and finely ribbed vaults. Behind the château the Vale of the Amasse leads to Clos-Lucé, a little manor-house of brick and stone where Leonardo da Vinci lived during his last years. Toward the south jutting above the woods, a curious pagoda stands where the lanes cross, reminding you of the pomp of Chanteloup castle, built by the Duke of Choiseul.

As it approaches Tours, the Loire Valley broadens as far as the banks of the Cher, forming a vast panorama. By their variety and richness, the plants growing on the hillsides justify by themselves the name of « garden of France ». In this region of fruit trees and vineyards, on sunny terraces you will aise see the palm tree, the eucalyptus, the orange tree and the holm Oak. The variety of plants in the Loire region contrasts with that of the plateau, which is less rich and less well-known. It has hidden treasures, however, along the roads skirting the secondary valleys.

At Rochecorbon, a little stream which we have already seen in the Blesois rejoins the Loire : it is the Cisse, which from Vouvray to Vernou flows through one of the most famous wine districts of the region. Its deep, narrow valley and an infinity of vales and glens are the heart of a Touraine too little known to outsiders. A detour at the place called « Vaufouinard » will lead you to a little castle. Lest in the depths of an immense and somewhat neglected wooded park, Jallanges is not easily reached. After having crossed a mossy lane, then two courtyards bordered with outbuildings, one discovers a building of the late fifteenth century in brick with stone cornerstones. The façade has broad mullioned windows let in it and is topped with high dormer windows whose pointed gables stand out against a slate roof. In the center, a small polygonal tower, crowned by an overhanging top floor, houses the spiral staircase that leads to the second floor and attic. The entire façade is decorated with a great number of sculptured motifs in the flowery style of late Gothic: an ogee arch with a terminal fleuron above the front door and sculpted ornaments holding the window moldings. The quality and variety of this amazing decoration are astonishing in this forgotten spot.

North of Jallanges, the manor-houses of La Côte, Valmer and La Vallière await the curious visitor who goes astray on a little road or who arrives by way of the river from downstream. Descending the valley of the Brenne you arrive at the gates of Tours, after a stop at the fortified farm of Meslay whose front gate and colossal tithing-barn call to mind the former wealth of the powerful abbey of Marmoutier. That important monastic center stands not far away on the right bank of the Loire. Of this group of buildings, founded by St. Martin, there remains only a very small part which escaped the demolition that took place at the beginning of the nineteenth century : the fortified gate of the Crosse, the chapel of the Seven Sleepers and the Tower of the Bells, as well as fragments of the outer wall. Recent digging has unearthed the foundations of a Gothic church which is said to have been the model for the cathedral of Tours.

Coming from Marmoutier, you see the capital of Touraine rise behind the island-strewn Loire : « Tours, like Venice, seems to emerge from the waters »; but today it is more difficult to see what Balzac was referring to. Although the changes brought about during past centuries and the bombardments of the last war have changed its appearance, the city of Tours is modern only on the surface. As soon as you leave the large central axis, fragments of the old city can be seen. A few restored blocks of the old quarter are a quite faithful reconstitution of the medieval city, such as Plumereau Square and Change Street. And you should wander through streets still untouched by restoration and whose names call to mind the daily life of former times : Broom Street, Crossbow Street and Three Desks Street.

The ancient Gallo-roman city of the Turones was encircled by an outer wall that is still to be seen enclosing the square where the amphitheater was situated and on which the first St. Gatien's cathedral was built. The religious metropolis, which counted sixty buildings in the fate fifteenth century, has certainly lost some of its power but a few churches remain : St. Gatien, whose construction lasted from the thirteenth to the sixteenth century, is the most beautiful of the group, and the little cloister of Psalette, next to it, is a delicate work of the early Renaissance.

The former abbey of St. Julian, once very vast, is reduced to a Gothic church with a Romanesque belfry-porch and very thoroughly remodelled monastic buildings. But it is St. Martin's collegiate church, a famous place of pilgrimage during the Middle Ages, which has suffered most from destruction and indifference. All that remains today are two stately towers and some scattered vestiges in the neighborhood. Among these, a cloister dating from the early Renaissance evokes by its lavish sculpture the splendor of the art of the Loire region. The first great period of secular constructions is situated in the fifteenth and sixteenth centuries when Tours was a royal city. The city's prosperity was seen in the new structures : houses and private mansions built by rich merchants turned financiers to the king. The last war destroyed these buildings in part ; those remaining are often very much restored. Of the Beaune-Semblençay mansion there remains only a gallery wall and a fountain. After the bombardments, only the façade of the Goüin mansion was left and it had to be rebuilt stone by stone. Sometimes, walking at random through the streets, one sees a few mansions : Binet, Robin-Quantin, Babou de la Bourdaisière and the curious brick house wrongly called « Tristan ». These houses, which were built by rich burgers, were of stone, while the more democratic heart of the medieval city was built of brick and wood. Tours was at this period a flourishing city and an artistic captial : painters, sculptors, tapestry-makers and glassmakers, natives of the region or professionals attracted by the pre-sence of the king, produced their best works here.

The second period of construction is situated around the eighteenth century when the « stone bridge » was built and the great north-south opening was effected which completely changed the appearance of the medieval city. But it is the mansions of the seventeenth and eighteenth centuries that have most suffered from the bombardments of the last war and then from the reconstruction. The Mame mansion is now one of the rare examples of classical architecture in Tours.

A short distance from the city, between the Loire and the Cher, a little house of brick and stone flanked by a small tower is all that remains of the Plessis-lès-Tours castle. As soon as he was crowned, Louis XI showed his preference for this residence which was more a country house than a sinister fortified castle born of the romantic imagination of Sir Walter Scott. Nearby on the banks of the Loire, the priory of St. Cosmas, now restored, stands beside the ruins of one of the region's oldest Romanesque churches. The fifteenth-century priory quarters call to mind the last years of Ronsard who is buried in this garden of roses and box-trees.

On the opposite bank, facing St. Cosmas, St. Cyr hill rises above the Loire. The steepness of the cliff is masked by the abundant vegetation, a natural setting of greenery, dotted with villas and country houses. One of them is Grenadière where Balzac sometimes stayed.

After Tours, the right bank of the river is marked by an impressive number of châteaux and manor-houses as far as the junction with the Vienne. On Fondettes hill the manor-house of Chatigny, which can be seen from the levee, is a simple fate fifteenth-century structure of checkered brick and stone. The polychromy of its materials is current in the Loire Valley, especially between Luynes and Fondettes, and even modest houses use this technique on the upper floors, chimneys and gables. This decoration is sometimes used along with ornaments of the early Renaissance, as in Vieilles Ligneries manor-house. Near the lush green valley of the Choisille, this pretty sixteenth century building protects its solitude, far from curious visitors. How could you imagine that behind this unpretentious farm is hidden the « country house » of a hunamistic man of the Church?

On the right bank of the Loire between Chatigny and Luynes, the tufa cliff is perforated with cave dwellings as far as Luyne castle, which is built on a rocky spur. It is a stern fortress which commands from the top of its eight towers the Valley road and access to the plateau and which served as a look-out post to detect invaders coming from the river. Another witness to a warlike past is Cinq-Mars-la-Pile. You can still see in the park,

among the filled-in moats which have been turned into gardens, two towers razed to the « height of infamy » on Richelieu's orders. It is well known that brilliant young Cinq-Mars, the friend of Louis XIII, was himself beheaded for treachery.

Between Cinq-Mars-la-Pile and Langeais, the road follows the Loire, which spreads out here in all its splendor, swollen by the waters of the Cher. It now attains its fuit volume, flowing abundantly and stretching out many arms to embrace islands covered with thick pastureland and water-willow beds. Langeais castle, situated in the center of the town, seems the very image of the medieval castle of out childhood history books : a massive fortress with bare walls topped with machicolations and a watchpath, and whose thick towers defend it from all aggressions. The addition, in the nineteenth century, of a rather fantastic drawbridge, adds to the illusion. Built by Louis XI, this castle should have been one of those bastions that militarily boit in a province. Unfinished because useless and inefficient after the progress made in artillery, it is one of the last great fortresses.

Not far from Langeais, to the north, is a Renaissance château which is deserted and forgotten by all and whose existence is not even suspected by most Touraine people because it is not easy to get to : of Hommes, hidden in the bend of a fane near a farm, there remain today only ruins surrounded by running water. An inobservant passerby will hardly see it, overgrown as it is by vegetation, brambles, ivy and vines climbing over the stones. A wormeaten door leads to the inner courtyard. Although the château is completely ruined, one may find under the Virginia creeper some sculpted foliage, a scallop shell or the capital of a column worthy of Azay-le-Rideau. The arcades of an open gallery are assaulted by vines and eider branches. What was the fate of this building, the causes of its ruin? All these questions remain unanswered for its history is unknown to us.

You will return to the Loire after Langeais, opposite Bréhémont where river shad and salmon fishers still drap their nets. Here time flows smoothly and a last ray of sunlight lingers on the still boats in the evening splendor. This landscape of great delicacy is one of the most beautiful in Touraine.

The Touraine of the Old Regime ended at Langeais. Today its territory extends to the Bourgueil wine district and its environs. The Loire levee, from Langeais to Bourgueil, is edged below with an uninterrupted row of dazzlingly white houses. Sheepmen's houses, vine-growers' small-holdings, market gardens, all are carefully built of this beautiful building stone which becomes slightly pink in the sun. On the vine-covered slopes of the softly

rounded hillocks, the château of Benais can be seen behind the trees ; rebuilt in the last century, it retains from the former edifice a Renaissance entrance pavilion.

The village of Restigné has a few outstanding houses, symbols of the wine district's affluence and pleasant way of life. At its center, Bourgueil has kept the memory of a celebrated Benedictine abbey and still owns a parish church with beautiful Angevin vaults.

At the next stop we shall visit the little château of Réaux which was built in the early sixteenth century by a member of a great Touraine family, the Briçonnets. This Renaissance structure is in reality only a small castle whose walls are entirely made of brick and stone. But here the materials alternate imaginatively and humorously in different designs : checkerboards, zigzags and herringbones. It is an unexpected decorative minglement.

Touraine ends at Réaux, but the landscape on the banks of the Loire hardly changes until Saumur : there are few outstanding buildings except for a series of white houses built along the levee.

VALLÉE DE LA LOIRE
VALLEY OF THE LOIRE

1. La Loire à Orléans
1. The Loire at Orléans

2. *le château et l'église Jeanne d'Arc de Gien*
2. *Gien, castle and Jeanne d'Arc's church*

3. *La Bussière : château des XV-XVIe s. Musée de la pêche*
3. *La Bussière : château of the fifteenth and sixteenth centuries.*
Museum of Fishing

4 | 5 | 6
        | 7

*4/5. Saint-Benoît-sur-Loire : basilique romane
(XIe-XIIIe s.). Clocher-porche et chapiteau
(détail)*
*4/5. Saint-Benoît-on-Loire : Romanesque
basilica (eleventh to thirteenth century)*

*6. Château de Bellegarde : le donjon du XVIe s.,
cantonné d'échauguettes et entouré de douves*
*6. Bellegarde Castle : the fourteenth century
keep, flanked by watch turrets and surrounded
by a moat*

7. Le château de Chamerolles (XV-XVIIe s.)
*7. Chamerolles Castle (fifteenth to seventeenth
century)*

8 | 9

8. *Église de Germigny-des-Prés. Mosaïque byzantine (XIe s.) : déta [...] de l'Arche d'Alliance*
8. *Church of Germigny [...] of the Fields. Byzantine [...] mosaic (eleventh centu [...]*

9. *Église de Jargeau*
9. *The church of Jargea [...]*

10. Église Saint-Liphard de Meung-sur-Loire
10. St. Liphard's church of Meung-on-Loire

11. Château de Meung-sur-Loire
11. Meung-on-Loire Castle

12. *La Loire à Beaugency*
12. *The Loire at Beaugency*

13. *Château de Ménars : statue dans le parc*
13. *Château of Ménars : statue in the park*

14. Château de Ménars vu de la rive gauche de la Loire
14. Château de Ménars seen from the left bank of the Loire

18 | 19

Coucher de soleil sur le château de Chambord
Sunset over the château of Chambord

20. *Château de Chambord :*
le grand escalier
20. *Château of Chambord :*
the great staircase

21. *Château de Chambord :*
personnage de la terrasse
21. *Château of Chambord :*
figure on the terrace

23. Château de Chambord : la chambre du roi
23. Château of Chambord : the king's room

◄ *22. La forêt de Chambord vue de la terrasse du château*
22. Chambord forest seen from the terrace

24. *Château de Chambord : la chambre de la reine*
24. *Château of Chambord : the queen's room*

25. *Château de Chambord et son reflet dans le Cosson* ▶
25. *Château of Chambord and its reflection in the Cosson*

29. *Château de Blois :*
façade Louis XII
29. *Château of Blois :*
Louis XII façade

30. *Château de Blois : l'escalier François Ier*
30. *Château of Blois : staircase François I, detail*

31. *Château de Blois : la façade des loges*
31. *Château of Blois : façade of the loggias*

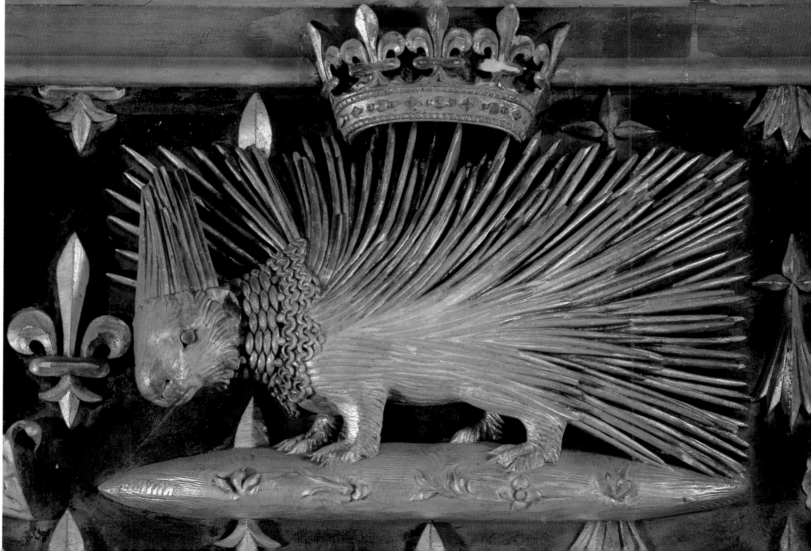

32. *Château de Blois : détail de cheminée, la salamandre attribut de François Ier*
32. *Château of Blois : detail of the chimney, the salamander, emblem of François I*

33. *Château de Blois : le porc-épic, attribut de Louis XII*
33. *Château of Blois : the porcupine, emblem of Louis XII*

34. *Château de Blois : les armoires secrètes du cabinet de Catherine de Médicis*
34. *Château of Blois : the secret closets of Catherine de' Médici's study*

35 | 36

35. *Vue aérienne du château de Chaumont-sur-Loire*
35. *Aerial view of Chaumont-on-Loire Castle*

36. *Château de Chaumont-sur-Loire : la chambre de Ruggieri*
36. *Chaumont-on-Loire Castle : Ruggieri's room*

◀ *37 Château de Chaumont-sur-Loire*
37 Chaumont-on-Loire Castle

38 Amboise : la ville et le château
38 Amboise : the city and the castle

39 | 40

39. Château d'Amboise : la cheminée de la salle des États
39. Château of Amboise : chimney in the Hall of the Estates

40. Château d'Amboise : la chambre de Louis-Philippe
40. Château of Amboise : Louis-Philippe's room

41	42
43	44

41. Amboise : la chapelle Saint-Hubert, détail du linteau
41. Amboise : St. Hubert's chapel, detail of the lintel

42. Manoir du Clos-Lucé
42. Clos-Lucé Manor

43/44. Manoir du Clos-Lucé : maquettes de machines réalisées d'après des dessins de Léonard de Vinci
43/44. Clos-Lucé Manor : models of machines constructed from Leonardo da Vinci's plans

45 | 46

45. Plessis-lès-Tours : voûte de la tour
45. Plessis-lès-Tours : vault of the tower

46. Tours : les verrières de la cathédrale Saint-Gatien (XIIIᵉ-XVᵉ)
46. Tours : the stained glass window of St. Gatien's cathedral (thirteenth to fifteenth century)

THE ANJOU

To enter the Vale of Anjou it is preferable to take the left bank, crossing the Loire at Port-Boulet, in order to arrive a little to its west at its junction with the Vienne at Candes-Saint-Martin. The countryside is more varied and picturesque and many edifices catch your attention.

The village of Candes calls to mind St. Martin who often retired to this hermitage. The curious fortified twelfth-century church, built on the site of the saint's cell, is worth a visit. The porch opening onto the Loire is surprising and the massive bare wall is enlivened by small columns and statues which unite Romanesque austerity to fine Angevin-style decoration. This elegance is found again inside the church where a delicate monolithic column holds the ribs of highly segmented vaults. The village, whose ancient houses hang from the hillside and gather around the church and a little turreted castle, overlooks the vast panoramam of the junction of the Loire and the Vienne.

Between Candes and Montsoreau, the narrow road running along the Loire is bordered with buildings that are for the most part very old and bear witness to the past wealth of the region. Montsoreau, situated between the hill and the river that formerly washed its walls, presents its façade to the sun. In spite of the watchpath with machicolations, no sign of austerity can be seen on its golden stone walls. Curious two-storeyed dormer windows decorated with pinnacles and crockets let light into the high attic. The inner façade is embellished with a staircase tower decorated with a strange bas-relief : above a recumbent deer, two monkeys hold a cask of wine and a banner with the lord's motto : « I Will do it ».

The road that follows the Loire from Montsoreau to Saumur has shady banks overlooked by a steep hill. Above a crag a village is hall-hidden in the greenery, a church timidly points its steeple, a manor-house is hiding. The unpretentious church of Parnay clings to the top of the cliff, while Souzay manor, a little fifteenth-century structure, leans its crenelated towers against the rock.

The abbey of Fontevraud is very close. Founded in the early twelfth century by Robert d'Arbrissel, it united two distinct communities of men and women under the direction of an abbess. The role played by the abbey in the monastic life of the medieval Western world explains the great size of its buildings. The abbatial church is no doubt, since the ruin of the collegiate church of St. Martin of Tours, the region's masterpiece of Romanesque architecture. The nave, which is covered with a very finely proportioned vault, is related to the Romanesque tradition of southwestern France. In the transept one discovers a fine example of medieval statuary : recumbent statues on the tombs of the Plantagenets who made Fontevraud their necropolis.

Leaving Fontevraud one returns to the Loire by a winding path : the valley of the Thouet, on the Touraine-Anjou border, is a perfect setting for a romantic walk. The course of this little stream continues, tortuous and narrow, to Saumur, crossing a countryside thickly dotted with manor- houses. At Montreuil-Bellay the river encloses the steep hill bearing the castle that is formed of a disorderly group of walls, ruins and disparate structures. Built in the fifteenth century, it is composed of four blocks of living quarters with staircase turrets, a haphazard juxtaposition which the visiter finds charming because it evokes the traditional feudal residence. The road running along the Thouet leads to Saumur, which, like Blois, should be viewed from the opposite bank of the Loire. The fifteenth-century town hall on the riverbank which is flanked by watch turrets, and the sharp steeple of St. Peter's church capture our attention less than the enormous mass of the castle overlooking the city. Situated on a hilltop, it occupies a place comparable to that of Amboise. Its high white façades and towers with pointed roofs call to mind the celebrated miniatures of the *Very Rich Hours of the Duke of Berry*. Unfortunately, the decoration of the dormer windows and the delicate superstructures that embellished the upper floors and the roof have disappeared. Today we must try hard to imagine the country house dear to King René.

In town another house, the mansion of the Queen of Sicily, with its beautiful flamboyant dormer windows, was built by King René's mother, Yolanda of Aragon. Nearby, there are few structures on the right bank except for Boumois castle, built on the bank of the Authion whose course here is parallel to that of the Loire. Partly rebuilt in the fifteenth century, it appears from behind a leafy fane. The buildings are disposed simply ; the main body of the building overlooks two lower wings. A water-filled moat surrounds it on all sides. Like Amboise, it is a castle whose rich flamboyant decoration illustrates the

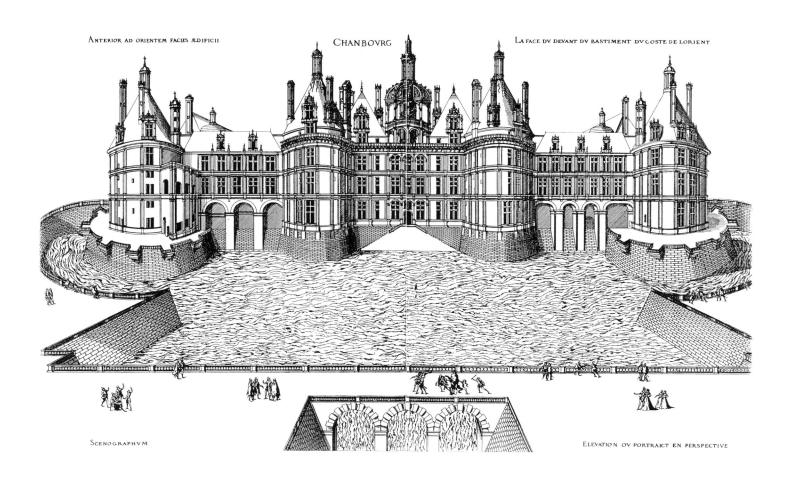

ANTERIOR AD ORIENTEM FACIES ÆDIFICII

CHANBOVRG

LA FACE DV DEVANT DV BASTIMENT DV COSTE DE LORIENT

SCENOGRAPHVM

ELEVATION OV PORTRAICT EN PERSPECTIVE

EIVSDEM FACIES POSTERIOR PRECEDENTI OPPOSITA AD OCCIDENTEM

CHANBOVRG

LA FACE DV DERRIERE DV MESME BASTIMENT OPPOSITE A LA PRECEDANTE DV COSTE DE LOCCIDENT

SCENOGRAPHVM

ELEVATION OV PORTRAICT EN PERSPECTIVE

short moment when Italianism had not yet came to France,

For us to reach Angers, the left bank is much more charming because of its landscape and its buildings.

At Trèves a colossal keep thirty meters (100 feet) high juts out over the Loire. Cunault, the neighboring village, is celebrated for its beautiful Romanesque church, the younger sister of Vézelay and St. Benedict's. Its construction took place from the eleventh to the thirteenth century. You can appreciate the tall, graceful proportions of the building and the depth of the nave, accentuated as it is by the shortening of the central hall. The indirect lighting which cames from the narrow openings of the side aisles, softly shapes the volumes and gives them an amazing fullness.

The surrounding countryside permits us to make other discoveries : the Romanesque church of St. Cosmas's priory and the outbuildings of Pimpéan castle. In the Valley of the Layon is one of the most beautiful castles of the region, Brissac. Its curious façade appears incoherent, the unfinished reconstruction showing the contributions of successive owners. Two great towers with machicolations, the vestiges of a fifteenth-century castle, frame a great seventeenth-century entrance pavilion decorated with bossing. But unity is maintained by the use of the same materials : schist for the walls and building stone for the tics. Inside is a monumental majestic staircase, one of the noblest in France.

To the south, in the direction of Cholet, Basse-Guerche and Lavouer are typically Angevin manor-houses. As at Brissac schist replaces tufa, which is reserved for the corner stones and window and door frames. With the change of material begins the passage to another region : to the south, the region of Mauges, land of the Chouans, announces the Vendée. We see the Loire again at Ponts-de-Cé, near a castle built by King René. All that romains of it is a keep crowned by a watchpath.

Then from Rochefort to Chalonnes the twisting road rises, crossing the vineyards in terraces above the Loire. Opposite the junction with the Layon, on the right bank, the « coulee of Serrant » shelters the castle of the same name. Less grandiose than Brissac, it unites harmoniously a Renaissance structure with classical decoration. In the middle of a large romantic park a beautiful pond holds up a mirror of water to the façades.

On the same bank, to the west, a ruined tower, traditionally attributed to Gilles de Rais, seems balanced on a schist crag like a bastion turned toward Britanny. This will be our last stop in the Vale of the Loire. Beyond, another country begins. This is the road to the sea, made detectable by a slight nuance of light and by the rising wind. The landscape is harsher, the Vale narrows and the Loire now flows between high granite walls.

And yet, on the left bank, two small buildings call to mind the Angevin gentleness sung by the poet. At Liré, the native region of Joachim du Bellay, stands the chapel of Bourgonnière : this jewel of the Renaissance is like a goodbye to the Loire Valley.

We couldn't leave Anjou, however, without stopping in its capital. Angers is the only city built away from the river. Contrary to Blois and Tours it does not occupy a site that can be taken in at a glance. The castle's mass and that of the cathedral on the edge of the hill hide the old city.

This castle, a formidable fortress built by St. Louis, would appear more imposing if its towers had not been lowered. Inside, the « châtelet » or « little castle » is in fact a country house which calls to mind the memory of King René. St. Maurice's cathedral is the most original Gothic church in France : its single nave is covered with a high-pitched vault, halfway between the traditional pointed vaults and cupolas, a striking testimony of the Angevin Gothic style. It formerly contained the celebrated Apocalypse tapestries which are now in the castle. It is well known that they were made in the fourteenth century for Louis I of Anjou by Nicolas Bataille according to drawings by Hennequin of Bruges.

Several famous churches and abbeys remain around the cathedral. The choir of St. Sergius's church is a masterpiece of the Angevin Gothic style. St. Aubin's abbey has kept only its cloister, now situated inside the perimeter walls of the prefecture. Its arcades are decorated with painted scenes ; the finesse and precision of the design are in keeping with the freshness of the colors. In the quarter beyond the Maine, St. John's hospital, a vast medieval block that has been transformed into a museum, houses tapestries by Lurçat. Ronceray abbey close by is aise an interesting example of Angevin art.

Angers is one of those provincial capitals that remain pleasant towns but can be understood only from the inside. Like those of Bourges and Blois, Angers's old quarter is quite homogenous and well-integrated into the framework of daily life and has not been excessively restored. Fine fifteenth- and sixteenth-century houses fine the streets where you still see old signs : Adam's house and the one of the beautiful Angevin woman, the Pincé mansion and the Barrault house. On the other side of the Maine, the former home of the Penitents surprises you by the refinement of its Renaissance decoration which is quite unexpected in such a building. But at Angers, the main part of the old quarters is made up of seventeenth- and eighteenth- century mansions which bear witness to the city's prosperity at the end of the Old Regime.

Angers is situated a little back from the Vale of the Loire at the junction of three streams which meet in a single arm, the Maine. The streams, the Sarthe, the Mayenne and the Loir, all flow through wooded districts before meeting. Lush green meadows make of the region surrounding Angers a land of incomparable freshness, dotted with many castles. We shall give no itinerary here, for the pleasure of discovery results from a certain imagination being exercised as you walk along. A few castles should be seen for their typically regional character or for their architectural interest. Northeast of Angers, here is Plessis-Macé, on the bank of the Mayenne. In the fate fifteenth century, on the site of a former fortress were built elegant structures crowned with pronouncedly overhanging upper floors. The whimsical plan of the building is not lacking in charm, and the variations in level of the roofs, the jagged silhouette of the steep gables and the high dormer windows accentuate its medieval aspect. In the main courtyard St. Michael's chapel has retained its gallery with open-work from the flamboyant period, a rare and precious model of fate fifteenth-century wooden architecture.

The lover of architecture cannot be unaware of Plessis-Bourré castle on the banks of the Sarthe. It is one of the most important and best-preserved buildings in France from the second hall of the fifteenth Century. Built by Jean Bourré at the same time as Langeais, it was finished in 1473. Although still feudal in conception, with its broad moat and its defensive apparatus, the plan of the buildings announces a new day. The lower perimeter wall allows one to see the seigniorial living quarters situated at the back of the courtyard and opening widely onto the outside world ; on the side, an open gallery links the chapel to the main part of the building. In opposition to Langeais, which is still rooted in feudal tradition, Plessis-Bourré affirms a new concept of the nobleman's residence ; the disposition of the building, which was revolutionary at the time, was to exert a great influence on constructions in the Vale of the Loire during the sixteenth century.

Before we leave Anjou, a last walk will lead us to Montgeoffroy, east of Angers. This château, of great simplicity, unrolls its long, white façade at the end of a fane. Field Marshal de Contades built it in the 1750s. The apartments contain a unique set of eighteenth-century furniture, which has never been dispersed, a circumstance rare in France. The chapel prolonging the right wing belonged to the earlier sixteenth- century structure.

The gate with its pointed arch, a beautiful octagonal bell- tower and especially a superb Renaissance stained glass window do not belie its reputation as Anjou's most handome seigniorial chapel.

Compared to Touraine and to the Blesois, Anjou is no doubt less rich in great castles, having ton at the most.

But if one lingers here, one finds a countryside rich in beautiful residences which are more familial than princely. They express with grace, poetry and tenderness the soul of the region.

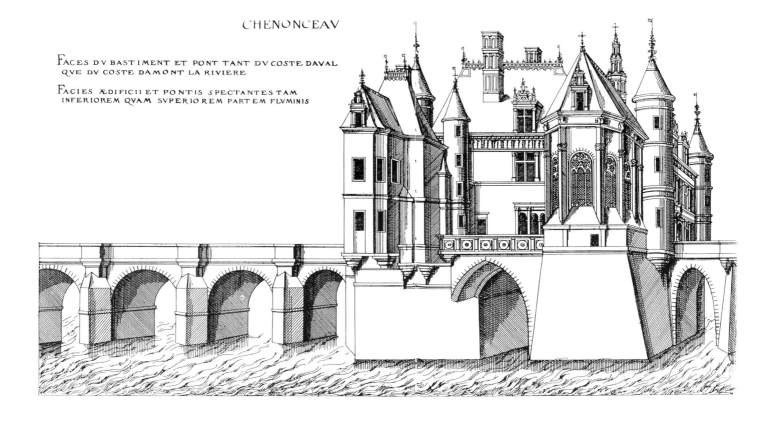

CHENONCEAV

FACES DV BASTIMENT ET PONT TANT DV COSTE DAVAL
QVE DV COSTE DAMONT LA RIVIERE

FACIES ÆDIFICII ET PONTIS SPECTANTES TAM
INFERIOREM QVAM SVPERIOREM PARTEM FLVMINIS

47. Château des Réaux
47. Les Réaux Castle

49. *Château de Langeais*
49. *Langeais Castle*

50. *Église de Gizeux : priant. La femme de René du Bellay en costume Henri IV*
50. *Church of Gizieux : person praying. The wife of René du Bellay in a Henri IV period costume*

◄ 48. *Château de Langeais : tapisserie flamande, la Crucifixion*
48. *Langeais Castle : flemish tapestry, The Crucifixion*

54. Le confluent de la Loire et de la Vienne à Candes-Saint-Martin
54. Junction of the Loire and the Vienne at Candes-Saint-Martin

63 | 64

63. Château de Brissac :
le plafond de la salle des
Gardes
63. Château of Brissac :
the ceiling of the guardroo

64. Château de Serrant :
la bibliothèque
64. Château of Serrant :
the library

73. Voûtes du chœur de l'église Saint-Serge d'Angers
73. The vault of the choir of St. Serge's church of Angers

2

THE VALLEYS

CHER, INDRE, INDROIS, CREUSE, VIENNE, LOIR

The Vale of the Loire can be dissociated neither from the valleys of its great tributaries, at least in their lower courses, nor from the many vales where small streams flow. The tight network of secondary valleys constitutes, south of the Loire especially, an attractive natural setting. Two of these rivers bear two châteaux which could by themselves sum up the art of the Loire : Chenonceau astride the Cher and Azay-le-Rideau enclosed in a trop of the Indre. But beside these wonders, how many more modest or less known edifices, how many towns with evocative names: Montrichard, Loches and Chinon are the most famous and the richest in medieval history.

Southward, three rivers join the Loire between Tours and Candes, cutting up the arid Touraine plateau with little cases of greenery and running water and giving this province its particular look. Northward, the Loire flows through a broad plain and meanders from Vendôme to Angers, constituting the natural border between the regions of the Loire, the western wooded district and Beauce.

Each drains a little bit of the country it crosses. In Berry the Cher is still just a rough draft of itself south of the Blesois but becomes more sedate in Touraine in a broad valley. The Indre, more rapid and wandering, flows through a valley that is sometimes deep and narrow, always green and broken up by dams and mills. The Vienne, coming from Poitou, receives in Touraine a tributary from the mountains, the Creuse, then becomes slow and lazy near Chinon and its junction with the Loire. To understand the deep and often unexpected charm of these valleys, we must leave the main highways and wander over the many little roads that run along beside the streams. All have inspired artists and incited builders to construct beautiful castles on their banks. They are more than ornaments to these streams; they are a sort of musical accompaniment.

3

THE CHER VALLEY

Before approaching the Cher Valley in its lower region, we must not forget Bourges and Upper Berry which have a particular place in the « Art of the Loire ». Like Tours and Blois, Bourges has benefitted from circumstances favorable to its artistic flowering. In the fourteenth century the duchy was detached from the crown and became the domain of Jean de Berry who made of Bourges an artistic center unique in France. Later Charles VII inherited his property. Bourges then became the point of departure for the conquest of the English-occupied kingdom. Installed in the castle of Mehun-on-Yèvre, nearby, the king received the financial support of Jacques Cœur, the richest man in the kingdom. In the fate Middle Ages Bourges became an economic and intellectual conter, attracting and holding great fortunes and artists. To these historic factors is added the particular geographical position of this border region between the north and the south of France, favorable to all kinds of exchange.

From the medieval period Bourges has kept a splendid cathedral, one of the finest examples of French Gothic architecture. Its unique plan is not lacking in originality the double side aisles of decreasing height allow the openings to be arranged in tiers and permit a distribution of the light that transforms the building into a real greenhouse. An exceptional set ofthirteenth- to sixteenth-century stained glass windows accentuates the wonder one feels and creates, by the variety of colors, a light that is completely unreal.

The fate fifteenth and early sixteenth centuries have left, in the field of secular architecture, many examples of the prosperity and wealth of the town. The best known is, of course, the mansion built by Charles VII's financier, the unfortunate Jacques Cœur. And yet a few Renaissance residences, like the Cujas mansion and especially the Lallemand mansion, are, by the refinement of their sculpted decoration, the equals of their Touraine and Blesois counterparts.

In general, the old city has kept its integrity, more even than Blois. Established on a hillside overlooked by the cathedral, hall-timbered houses alternate there with handsome mansions set in gardons.

In the immediate environs of the city, one finds a great many buildings worthy of attention, churches, castles and abbeys, among which it is difficult to choose. Romanesque art is particularly well represented in Berry, with the celebrated abbeys of Noirlac and Chezal-Benoît and several churches that are more modest but have abundant sculpted decorations, like those of Plaimpied and Germigny-l'Exempt. The castles of Berry long remained faithful to the Gothic tradition, as they embellished their inner walls with luxurious and flowery decorations, of which the finest example is probably Meillant.

Northeast of Bourges, between the Loire and the Sauldre, several small castles, most of them unknown, are worth mentioning : Boucard, Blancafort, Pezeau and Buranlure, with their musical names. If I had to select one it would be Verrerie, a few miles from La-Chapelle-d'Angillon, the country of « grand Meaulnes ». It is situated in a forest, facing an immense pond, on the melancholy site that inspired Alain Fournier. Built in the early sixteenth century of brick and stone, it unites the delicate colors of the materials with the refinement of the sculpted decorations. Precious in appearance, it seems like a product of Italy in the middle of stern Berry. Not far from there, Aubigny-sur-Nère, a one-street village, situated on the border of Sologne, surprises us by a series of hall-timbered houses. The Gare given to these structures as well as a recent restoration give this country village a peculiar appearance which makes it seem to have come out of a Grimm's fairy tale.

At Vierzon, the Cher begins its lower course and leaves Berry to skirt the south of the Blois region before entering Touraine. Still choppy in Berry, it becomes calmer near the Loire. Its broad valley bordered with low hills is not very picturesque but it is nonetheless not monotonous. The market gardons and the meadows are broken up by rows of alders and poplars which are filled with birds on sunny days. The horizon is limited on either side by gentle slopes covered with vineyards.

The passage from Berry to the Blesois occurs alter the fortified village of Mennetou at Selles-on-Cher, formerly known as Selles-in-Berry. The town has two castles on the same site: the first one, of the fourteenth century, replaced a former fortress; the second, which is unfinished, was built in the seventeenth century by Philippe de Béthune, Sully's brother. Opposite its entrance, the Romanesque church possesses the singularity of a double sculpted frieze which ornaments the entire apse wall.

At Romorantin the Cher welcomes the Sauldre, a slow, lazy stream from Sologne which is broken up by ponds. It was here that Francis I spent his childhood and planned to build his dream palace, before deciding on Chambord. Sauldre demarcates, together with the Beuvron, a little wooded region which effects the transition from Sologne to the Blois region, where the density of castles is great. The largest and best known is Cheverny, a huge residence of the seventeenth century, which is situated in a park with magnificent foliage. Cheverny is one of the rare Loire castles that still belongs to a descendant of the family that owned it in the sixteenth century : Hurault de Vibraye de Cheverny.

The structure we see today was built in 1634 on the site of a sixteenth-century manor-house. It is composed of a high and narrow central rectangular block flanked by two square pavilions with lantern-turrets on their roofs. The interest of Cheverny lies also in the interior decoration of Louis XIII period panelling with paintings representing Don Quixote's life and with Gobelin tapestries.

More modest, but equally attractive, are the manor-houses of Chémery, Herbault, Moulin and Morinière. The castle of Moulin, built on a terrace surrounded by broad ditches, has brick and stone façades ornamented with a black lozenge design. This rustic decoration, which is common in Sologne, is in no way inconsistent with a military apparatus that became useless in the fate fifteenth century.

More recent, but having the same character, its neighbor, La Morinière, presents to the sun its pink brick walls and towers reflected by the stagnant waters of a pond. In the heart of a village, Fougères, a stocky fortress, seems to have been placed there on the square since its moat was filled in. An agreeable inner courtyard embellished by an open gallery and a staircase tower belies the harsh appearance of its outer wall.

Turning again toward the south we rejoin the Cher at Saint-Aignan; on the slopes this little town is overlooked by the château which was rebuilt in the sixteenth century. One arrives at the château from the Romanesque church by way of a stairway of 144 steps. The inner courtyard is closed on two sides by an L-shaped block of living quarters whose façades are adorned with superposed pilasters and dormer windows surmounted by high pediments. The other two sides of the terrace are bordered by a balustrade and open on a vast view of the valley. Near Saint-Aignan, on the left bank of the Cher, curious visitors will find the path leading to the ruins of Aiguevive Abbey.

Unconditional levers of old stones are

now trying to preserve these vestiges. But time is at work here and the building continues to deteriorate. In places, one can just barely see the outline of a fresco which will soon vanish completely. Between Saint-Aignan and Montrichard, the Cher takes in a stream with the amusing name of « Traine-Feuilles » (Drag-Leaves). It has its source in a forest surrounding Gué-Péan castle. At a bend in the fane one suddenly cames upon the castle set upon a softly rolling meadow. It is a structure of the sixteenth and seventeenth centuries in white stone with a slightly grey cast, but which a sunbeam can turn to pink. A little bridge astride a dry moat leads to the entrance gate flanked by truncated towers. The L- shaped living quarters, framed by two thick cylindrical towers, open onto a paved courtyard. In spite of the successive stages of constructions, Gué-Péan has kept a certain unity because of the beauty and luminosity of the stone. Without frills or any imposing feature, it is a charming place.

Following the course of the Cher, here we are at Montrichard, a medieval town built on the side of a chalky hill and crowned by a formidable square keep which rises in the midst of a pile of ruined ramparts and fortifications. To arrive there, you must climb to the upper city, which is constituted of semi-troglodytic habitations, paths, stairways and tiny hanging gardens.

From there, you overlook a beautiful landscape and in one glimpse you take in the Cher Valley as far as Touraine, as far as Chenonceau.

The road runs along the Cher at the fort of a cliff against which Chissay castle leans. Its Gothic façades, although very much remodelled, gracefully stand out against a cedar and plane-tree park.

Chenonceau owes its fame as much to its Renaissance architecture as to the originality of its location on the river. A long plane-tree avenue leads to the forecourt, then to the terrace, surrounded by a broad moat, on which still stands the keep of the Marques, the only primitive vestige. From the terrace, a few steps and a bridge lead to the château built in 1515 by Thomas Bohier on the piers of the former mill. It is a great square pavilion with turrets at the corners and whose façades date from the early Renaissance : openings framed by fluted pilasters, large dormer windows with pediments and candelabra. Inside, the straight staircase is the first of this style in the Loire Valley, along with the one at Bury castle, since destroyed. The château, become the property of the crown, was given to Diane of Poitiers by Henry II. We owe to her the bridge over the Cher which was to connect the graceful residende of Thomas Bohier to the other bank.

Catherine de' Medici afterwards built the two floors of the gallery on the bridge. Its already classical and somewhat academic sobriety contrast with the highly refined decor of the Renaissance pavilion. This surprising structure was designed to astonish people and was the setting of lavish parties given by the sons of Catherine de' Medici. Besides the magnificence and the luxury of the building, one is struck today by the calm and serenity surrounding it. To feel the subtle charm of this alliance of stone and water, you must see Chenonceau in the winter or spring when its only ornament is the fog that rises from the river.

No large houses are to be seen between Chenonceau and Tours, but you may discover off the beaten track a few structures which are sometimes full of memories : Beauvais, which was built in the eighteenth century and was during the First Empire the setting for some « shady business ». Its neighbor, Nitray, is a Renaissance manor-house whose gardens overlook the Cher. Each village that marks this road is richened by a church worthy of our interest or a forgotten building like the Romanesque priory of Saint-Jean-du-Grais.

Then the Cher flows along south of Tours and is completely canalized and broken up by reaches. It was still navi-gated here in the last century and a short canal connected it to the Loire, which it rejoins alter having lazily crossed a sometimes flooded plain. Near the junction with the Loire Vilandry stands at the fort of a hill in the middle of a garden in the French style whose flower beds are arranged in terraces in the style of Renaissance gardens. The construction of the castle shows some analogies with Villesavin, for it is also the work of Jean Le Breton. The complete restorations it underwent in the eighteenth century and later have made it lose all its Renaissance character. It was, however, like Villesavin one of the first castles to break with medieval tradition, the corner towers being replaced by square pavilions. It is regrettable that since the gardens have been reconstructed, the romantic park, which as at Ussé and Azay constituted a setting of greenery, has disappeared.

From the terraces, one sees the junction of the two rivers whose « spit », which was built up in the eighteenth century, preserves the valley from catastrophical high waters. Calmed and canalized, the place of junction is a strange country where arms of stagnant water bordered by dense vegetation mingle with dikes and dead-end paths.

VALLÉE DU CHER
VALLEY OF THE CHER

74. *Château de Cheverny : portrait d'Anne de Thou*
74. *Château of Cheverny : portrait of Anne de Thou*

75. *Château de Cheverny : portrait de Jeanne d'Aragon (atelier de Raphaël)*
75. *Château of Cheverny : portrait of Jeanne d'Aragon (Raphael's studio)*

76 | 77

76. Château de Meillant
76. Meillant Castle

77. Château de Meillant : portrait de Charles VII
77. Meillant Castle : portrait of Charles VII

◄ 78. Le Jugement dernier,
détail du portail de la cathédrale
Saint-Étienne de Bourges
78. The Last Judgement, *detail*
of the cathedral St. Étienne
of Bourges

79. Vitraux (XIIIe s.) de la
cathédrale Saint-Étienne
de Bourges
79. Thirteenth century stained
glass windows of St. Étienne
of Bourges

81 | 82

81. Château de Cheverny : détail de la cheminée de la chambre du roi
81. Château of Cheverny : detail of the chimney of the king's room

82. Château de Cheverny : la chambre du roi
82. Château of Cheverny : the king's room

◄ 80. Château de Cheverny
80. Château of Cheverny

83 | 84

83. *Château de Cheverny : portrait de la comtesse de Cheverny par Mignard*
83. *Château of Cheverny : portrait of the countess of Cheverny by Mignard*

84. *Château de Cheverny : le grand salon*
84. *Château of Cheverny : Great drawing room*

85 | 86

85. *Forêt de Lamotte-Beuvron*
85. *Lamotte-Beuvron Forest*

86. *La Ferté-Beauharnais : coucher de soleil sur l'étang*
86. *La Ferté-Beauharnais : sunset over the pond*

87. Lassay-sur-Croisne : le château du Moulin
87. Lassay-on-Croisne : Moulin Castle

93/94. Chenonceau : les deux façades du château
93/94. Chenonceau : the two façades of the château

95 | 96

95. *Château de Chenonceau : la galerie de Catherine de Médicis*
95. *Château of Chenonceau : Catherine de' Medici's gallery*

96. *Château de Chenonceau :* Les Trois Grâces, *de Van Loo, détail*
96. *Château of Chenonceau :* The Three Graces *by Van Loo, detail*

97. *Vue aérienne du château de Chenonceau* ▶
97. *Aerial view of the château of Chenonceau*

98. *Château de Chenonceau : la chambre de Catherine de Médicis*
98. *Château of Chenonceau : Catherine de' Medici's room*

99. *Château de Chenonceau : le cabinet de Diane de Poitiers*
99. *Château of Chenonceau : Diane de Poitiers's study*

100 | 101

100. *Château de Chenonceau : plafond du cabinet vert*
100. *Château de Chenonceau : ceiling of the green study*

101. *Château de Chenonceau : cabinet de nacre*
101. *Château of Chenonceau : mother of pearl room*

*Château de Villandry :
les jardins*
*Château of Villandry :
the gardens*

4

THE INDRE VALLEY

From the point of junction with the Cher the passage toward the Indre Valley is easy. The two rivers flow parallel to each other in the same vale. Contrary to the Cher, the Indre has no tributary. It is divided into a ramification of little arms separated by fines of poplars, willows and plane-trees.

On one of these arms stands Ussé opposite an immense valley which extends its alluvial plains beyond the Loire as far as the hill of Bourgueil. The castle is set at the base of a densely wooded, chalky cliff where it displays its white façades. The quality of the tufa gives the building an exceptional luminosity which is accentuated by the refinement of the decoration. More than a defensive castle, it seems to be the survivor of a bygone time, harmoniously uniting the various stages of its construction and remodelling. In the seventeenth century the feudal aspect was somewhat attenuated by opening the courtyard onto the valley. A set of terraces today clears the view and permits us to see from quite a distance this beautiful front façade whose delicate Gothic ornamentation, veritable damascening in stone, stands out against the forest.

At a short distance, the most refined of the châteaux of the Loire is situated on an island in the Indre, whose waters reflect its façades. Azay-le-Rideau, built from 1518 to 1527 by G. Berthelot, has remained unfinished : only two wings were built. The two blocks of living quarters, arranged in a right angle, open onto the main courtyard, which is flanked at the outer angles by corbelled towers which are crowned with false machicolations. It is the very type of the château of the Loire, with its feudal form and graceful Renaissance ornamentation.

The disposition of the façades demonstrates a set purpose of regularity which was obtained by the intersection of the super-imposed pilasters framing the openings and by the double set of moldings separating the floors. The decor romains reduced to the essentials, however, the pilasters, window rails and piers are bare and the sobriety of the walls brings out the preciosity of the sculpted features. They are of exceptional quality : capitals, dormer window pediments, foliage and especially the fine vertical section of the staircase forming a triumphal arch are set off by the simplicity of the walls. The Italian-type staircase is covered with coffered vaulting decorated with medallions. The balanced rhythm of the façades and the regular disposition of the structure demonstrate a sense of moderation rarely seen. It has often been said of Azay-le-Rideau that it is the most feminine of the châteaux of the Loire, because of its grace, its delicacy and the happy harmony which associates the beauty of its natural setting with the splendor of the edifice.

A pale imitation of Azay and probably of more recent construction, its neighbor, Islette, also stands on the banks of the Indre. If it had not suffered deplorable defacement during the last century, one could detect many analogies between the two structures, especially in the sculpted decoration.

Upstream from Azay, the Indre becomes more secret and less easily approached than the Cher ; it flows south of Tours in a more steep-sided valley and is often hidden behind a curtain of trees. It is choppy, sometimes rapid and broken by mills and dams, sometimes whimsical and slow, sprawling Dut in the middle of mea-dows in broad loops fuit of water lilies. Its banks, as well as the southerly plateau and secondary valleys, are a setting for many manor-houses and charming cottages, like that of Balzac at Saché and the manor-house of Vonnes, described by the writer under the name of Clochegourde in The Lily in the Valley.

The little castle (châtelet) of Thilouse surprises by its isolated situation in the middle of a field. Atone on the plateau, it is a small building composed of a square pavilion with four cylindrical towers at the corners. It stands on an island in the middle of a small pond which serves as a moat. The entrance through the northern façade is a semi-circular-arched door preceded by a fixed bridge which has replaced the drawbridge. Above the door, a pilastered window is surmounted by a dormer window whose pediment is decorated with a scallop shell. The surrounding garden, overrun with weeds and given over to brambles and underbrush, seems to be trying with its pitiful weapons to protect the mystery of this little castle. The history of this structure remains a mystery and it is only too natural that it has fallen into its present state.

Near Montbazon, the Indre Valley narrows between two picturesque and sometimes steep hills. On a crest above the trees and roofs of the village, a keep shored up by rounded buttresses dominates the valley with its mass.

On the edge of the plateau, above the river, a handsome and solitary farm draws our attention. Its name atone is a poem : « The Beautiful Cane-Brake ». It seems to be standing in the middle of the fields, showing on the side of the country rather plain, low façades flanked by stocky round towers. The attics of the living quarters are lighted by large dormer windows with sculpted pediments, a surprising thing in this rustic residence. The charm of Touraine often lies in these discoveries, but how many refined homes, symbols of a bygone way of life, are peasant houses today !

The vast horizons of the plateau of Sainte-Maure slope toward the Indre Valley at Cormery, which was the birthplace of an abbey that was famous from the twelfth to the seventeenth century. Although ruined or largely spoiled by the different uses to which they have been put, the remains of the abbatial buildings are worth visiting. They are moreover considerable enough to allow us to make a mental reconstitution of the abbey. Strolling in the little streets, you will discover a tower, the arcades of a cloister, convent buildings and a deconsacrated abbatial church. Today the village sleeps among these vestiges, joining them to a tight network of homes in a setting of running water, broad meadows and graves.

The Indre receives, not far from there, a tumultuous and vagabond stream, the Indrois, whose valley will give us the occasion to run away and get lost!

5

THE INDROIS VALLEY

Perched at the meeting place of the two rivers, Follaine, a little manor-house of the fifteenth century, charms us by its name which is reminiscent of some folly. Down below the rapid Indrois rushes between ashes and service trees, swollen by the many streams that dash down from the plateau. In a splendid wooded glen little Montpoupon castle seems like a dream; a perhaps excessive restoration has changed it into a parody of a fortress.

L'Estang, isolated in a great forest, is better preserved : the fifteenth century residence is lighted by mullioned windows surmounted with high dormer windows with crockets. The side wing is adorned, as at Blois, with a gallery whose arcades are supported by twisted pillars. At the edge of this great forested area, the Indrois flows beside the ruins of the charter-house of Liget and the fortified house of Courroirie,

before crossing a more open valley. This valley is marked by villages typical of Touraine : Genillé, Saint-Quentin-on-Indrois and Villeloin-Coulangé which are each richened by a church, a château or a collegiate church. Sovereign of this tiny valley, Montrésor overlooks the Indrois from the cliff on which stands the castle built in the fifteenth century by Imbert de Bastarnay on the site of a fortress.

The very simple living quarters with high dormer windows retain an imposing, austere look marked by the Gothic tradition. The collegiate church, only a hundred meters (333 feet) away, contrasts with the castle by its handsome Renaissance style. Begun in the early sixteenth century, it was finished only in 1541, a tact that explains the alliance of traditional architecture and Italianized decoration. The gable has let into it a double door with depressed archways flanked by columns and surmounted by a row of niches with pillars. All these features are decorated with foliage, candelabra and arabesques whose low relief and delicate outlines call to mind the sculpted features of Azay-le-Rideau. The inside reminds us of an immense greenhouse where light flows in from the high windows, lighting up the recumbent statues on the tombs of the Bastarnays, in the back of the church. This collegiate church is one of the most remarkable examples of religious architecture of the early Renaissance in Touraine.

After Montrésor, the Indrois splits in places into several arms whose green valleys are broken up by wooded areas. Let's leave this hedge-lined path, cross the forest and so return to the banks of the Indre at Loches, a large and famous city in the valley. Laid out in tiers at the fort the castle, its silhouette is chopped up by turrets, bell-towers, sharp gables of living quarters bristling with dormer windows and ramparts. Centuries have passed over this city without leaving any deep marks or irremediable destruction, only wearing down here and there its old stones, and making them more gentle.

You enter the old town through the fortified gate of the Cordeliers (Franciscans), the vestige of the fifteenth- century perimeter watt. To the right, above more recent houses, rises St. Antony's Tower, a Renaissance bell-tower surmounted by a lantern-topped cupola ; at the upper end of « main street » one sees Picoys Gate and the front of the town hall among the hodge-podge of pointed roofs. The site of the castle, which is made up of the king's quarters, St. Ursus's (Saint-Ours) collegiate church and the former keep, overlooks the valley and crowns the city. This great block is surrounded by a jumble of high perimeter watts and curtain-watts overgrown with vegetation.

From the king's quarters, one can see as far as the great forest of Loches and toward the meadows on the banks of the Indre. The façades of the castle bear the trace of two phases in the royal construction : the first in the early fifteenth century, the second in a later century. The first living quarters have a crude military look, but the second block with its dormer windows and its ermine-tufted oratory is more attractive. This wing is flanked by a slim turret called the Agnes Sorel Tower, for it contains the young woman's tomb with her recumbent statue. Behind, at the highest part of the crag, St. Ursus's collegiate church points toward the sky its two spired towers and its two curious hollow octagonal pyramids. To the south, closing the perimeter wall, a formidable eleventh-century keep defies time. The old city at the foot of the castle, with its rows of houses chopped up by narrow streets, steep alleys and stairs, forms a rather picturesque maze. The fine of pointed gables is sometimes broken by a Renaissance façade like that of the Chancellery. Sixteenth-century structures are indeed rather rare at Loches. After the Hundred Years War, then the death of Charles VII, the kings forsook the town which went to sleep to dream of great times gone by.

Leaving Loches, we pass near the Renaissance château of Sausac on our way to Beaulieu-lès-Loches. Above the green pastures enclosed in the arms of the river, the spire of the twelfth-century abbatial church points to the sky. Of this Romanesque structure only the bell-tower and five arms of the transept remain, but St. Lawrence's chapel and several old-houses are still intact. To the south, the classical château of Verneuil stands on the bank of the Indre, its regular façades crowned with triangular pediments and a four-sided dome. It appears suddenly as you round a bend in the road, with a long lane of linden-trocs leading up to it. A few kilometers from there are found the important vestiges of the fortress of Bridoré. Here is an unexpected side of Touraine : that of military constructions, which enclose the province and which were built during the troubled times of the feudal period. It is a border region, more suited to defensive structures than to country houses. The Indre is from this point on a part of Berry, less moderato, wilder and more

tumultuous than in Touraine. It flows through a deep, narrow valley between grey limestone cliffs. On one of them you see Palluau, a small medieval town whose castle has handsome Gothic façades. In a less turbulent setting, Isle-Savary at Clion is one of the region's important buildings. Leaving the road by a dirt path, you will better appreciate the vast display of the living quarters around the main courtyard. Built in the fate fifteenth century, it is composed of a long rectangular pavilion with a square tower at each corner, one of them serving as keep. The entire building is crowned with a line of tall machicolations and retains its haughty defensive look.

The Indre and the Cher demarcate here a region rich in castles, of which the most famous is imposingly large Valençay. Situated on broad terraces overlooking the Nahon valley, it is a building dating from the second hall of the sixteenth century. It is composed of two large blocks of living quarters, arranged in an L-shape and connected by an enormous round tower crowned by a dame. Inside, the appartments enclose a handsome collection of Empire furniture. One hall is exclusively devoted to the historical souvenirs of the Prince of Talleyrand, who owned the château in the early nineteenth century.

In the park which extends westward from the château and slopes softly down to the valley, llamas, deer, cranes and flamingos run free. Its smaller, unknown neighbor, the château of Veuil, was no doubt much more precious and refined but it has suffered a great deal from being deserted. Of this Renaissance structure, only one wing remains, which has on the ground floor a gallery of low arcades whose decoration is comparable to that of the châteaux of the Loire.

The pearl of this border region between Touraine and Berry is uncontestably Argy. Built in the late fifteenth or early sixteenth century, it is a transition castle which unites Gothic tradition to the early beginnings of the Renaissance. As is the case at Meillant, it is enriched by surprising sculpted decorations : the façades of the inner courtyard, above the gallery, are studded with initials and flat fleur-de-lys. This original decoration evokes, by its finesse and precision, the work of a goldsmith.

At the gates of « black Berry », Argy still has some of the grace and light of the Loire which has strayed into this secret country described by the « lady of Nohant ».

Villegongis, an imperfect and late replica of Chambord, does not succeed in maintaining the illusion. In a melancholy setting of water and forests, it has nonetheless a particular charm when the autum wind drops on the mirror of the moat a thousand sequins of light. At Azay-le-Ferron one enters Brenne, a region of ponds and marshes, drowned in fog like Champeigne in Touraine.

VALLÉE DE L'INDRE
VALLEY OF THE INDRE

104. Vallée de l'Indrois entre Montrésor et Genillé
104. Indrois Valley between Montrésor and Genillé

108 | 109.
*Château
d'Azay-le-Rideau
Château
of Azay-le-Rideau*

110 | 111

110. Loches : portrait d'Agnès Sorel
110. Loches : portrait of Agnès Sorel

111. Château d'Azay-le-Rideau : Gabrielle d'Estrées au bain
111. Château of Azay-le-Rideau : Gabrielle d'Estrées bathing

112.
*Château
d'Azay-le-Rideau
Château
of Azay-le-Rideau*

113 | 114

113. Le donjon de Montbazon
113. The keep of Montbazon

114. Château de Valençay
114. Château of Valençay

115. *Loches illuminé : de gauche à droite, l'église Saint-Ours, le donjon, le Logis royal,*
la porte royale et la tour Saint-Antoine
115. *Loches illuminated : from left to right, St. Ours's church, the keep, the royal quarters,*
the royal gate and St. Antoine's tower

116 | 117

116. Montrésor : tours de
l'ancienne forteresse
116. Montrésor : towers
of the old fortress

117. Château de Villegongis
117. Château of Villegongis

6

THE CREUSE VALLEY

The passage between the valleys of the Creuse and the Indre is made by way of the Glaise and a network of secondary streams. The Glaise waters the small towns of Preuilly and Grand-Pressigny. One finds in the outskirts many important vestiges of workshops where flint was chipped and polished during the Stone Age. Preuilly, which is situated on a hill overlooking the river, is particularly rich in interesting monuments. One finds in a limited area a fifteenth-century castle, the ruins of a fortress, a collegiate church and a Romanesque abbatial church. Although the surrounding countryside is rather poor, one can still discover a few interesting things. On the road to Chambon, one sees Rouvray, a country seat typical of Touraine, which has undergone few changes since its construction.

The most important castle in the southern part of Touraine is Grand-Pressigny. It stands on an admirable site, protected by a square keep thirty-five meters (approximately 117 feet) high. The living quarters, which were built in the sixteenth century, are ligh-ted by high mullioned windows which are framed by columns with Ionic capitals. The vaulted gallery occupies the entire ground floor and opens onto the inner courtyard. Two tall slim turrets flank this block of living quarters, punctuating with a lighter note the stern façades. Inside, you can visit the museum of prehistory.

North of Preuilly, the Claise adds its waters to those of the Creuse, a mountain river which serves a natural boundary between Touraine and Poitou. Here a fortified castle, Guerche, built on the river banks, possesses an officient defensive apparatus with thick towers crowned with machicolations and, underground, its casemates. This place gives a certain image of the Touraine countryside: the quiet, tranquil village is unaware of passing time, grouped as it is around a château hidden behind the trees, and the river's calm mirror reflects the moving image of the façades and pointed roofs.

The Creuse flows by the cliffs of Poitou and widens its valley in the direction of Touraine. Southward, the hill is covered with woods and thick underbrush, while to the north, the terraces of grain and meadows rise gently to the edge of the plateau. Among the many small streams rushing down to the Creuse, one has a savory name: the Aigronne. Rocky spurs, which are somewhat unexpected in this region, frame it as they jut out over the aggressive sites where medieval fortresses stand. La Celle-Guenand and Chatelier are two fairly typical examples of military architecture. In grey weather they look like Rhenish burgs.

Near the « Spit of the Two Waters », the meeting place of the Creuse and the Vienne, the modest valley of the Esves is enriched by a more attractive structure.

The château of Sepmes, which was built in the sixteenth century, has suffered from being deserted for so long, but it is now coming back to life due to an intelligently made restoration. It was built by a minor lord of Touraine who was for a time the beneficiary of bath royal favor and royal gold. This protection explains the lavish character of the house. A handsome staircase still exists.

7

THE VIENNE VALLEY

Contrary to the Creuse, the Vienne flows through Touraine in a broad valley with softly sloping banks. The chalky ribs of the fairly distant and wood-bordered hills sometimes break through in patches, as at Chinon. But before crossing the Chinonais, the river flows beside the limestone plateau of Sainte-Maure. Its aridity and monotony are suddenly broken by the green countryside. In the midst of this setting so marked by gentleness and moderation, the small castle of Brou is well integrated. Although successive remodellings have changed the original character of this Gothic edifice, the general aspect has been preserved. The outer façade, which is, exceptionally for Touraine, the most elaborately decorated, opens onto the valley. The fortunate builders had understood that one could make use of the harmony of the countryside and the whiteness of the building materials.

The luminosity of the buildings, in this southerly part of Touraine, is due to the quality and caler of the stone. In the fifteenth and sixteenth centuries it came from a nearby quarry, located near Sainte-Maure in the Courtineau Valley. The slightly ocher ecru caler catches the sun and clothes the most modest structures in light. Thus appear the houses of a very small village located on the slope of a plateau whose view opens onto the Valley of the Vienne. Crissay-on-Manse, a protected site today, is a group of old well-preserved buildings which are built of the material usually used only for the houses of nobles. The traveller curious to discover Touraine may wander over the entire Valley of the Manse.

After Crissay, the hills become steeper around Roches-Tranchelions where ruins still remain of a Gothic castle and a Renaissance collegiate church. The church of the neighboring village, Avon-les-Roches, is a rather remarkable Romanesque edifice : its porch has semi-circular arcades, whose sculptured archivolts are supported by little columns with historiated capitals. This part of Touraine is rich in examples of Romanesque art : the

Benedictine abbey of Bois-Aubry, the ruins of St. Leonard's at Ile-Bouchard, the church of Parçay-on-Vienne. The latter has a front door whose curves are decorated with strange bearded figures alternating with foliage, palmettes, beading and nail-head ornamentation. The richness of this decoration reveals the proximity of Poitou, as at St. Leonard's where the capitals carved in the shape monsters call to mind those of Chauvigny.

And yet, in the south of Touraine the most important example of Romanesque art is the little church of Tavant. To the beauty of the sculpted decoration is added a group of perfectly preserved frescoes. The building has kept a great deal of charm due to the little cemetery that lies next to it and the beautiful lane that leads to the western façade. We enter through an arched doorway, flanked by blind arcades and topped with three elaborately decorated arches. In the nave several interesting capitals remain, but the frescoes of the crypt are the most curious part of the church.Scenes from the Old and New Testaments are to be seen side by side with those of secular inspiration ; the themes evoked, whether religious or not, are an inventory of universalist thought during the Romanesque period. You will appreciate the skill of the drawing which is accentuated by the use of a limited range of colors : ocher, green, white and black.

Overlooking the Valley of the Vienne upstream from Chinon, Brétignoles manor-house rises above a grassy slope. One sees this fine house behind a large iron gate framed by smaller gates for pedestrians. Among the many old houses in the Chinonais this is one of the best preserved. The living quarters, lighted by mullioned-windows and surmounted with dormer windows, are flanked by towers without machicolations. In the center of the façade, a polygonal staircase turret gives this manor-house the last touch necessary to make it look like a country home. Before Chinon, the alluvial terraces on either side of the Vienne are covered with vineyards and orchards. Ligré, Cravant and Panzoult, all charming little villages, are alse the names of great vintages of this wine country.

Then Chinon appears in the sun, stretching out on a chalky cliff the silhouette of its ruined castle. At its feet, the « little town of renown » extends from the cliff to the Vienne, forming a landscape of mainly horizontal fines. The vestiges of the three castles occupy a rocky spur overlooking the river, cut off on the south by a sheer cliff and limited on the north by a deep, narrow dale. The structures take the shape of this natural site and are arranged in a long complicated rectangle of fortifications and defensive works. Of the castle, which was demolished in the early nineteenth century, there remain only the vestiges we see today : the Clock Tower, Coudray Tower and Fort St. George ; you must make a great effort to imagine what the buildings were like. Coming from the town, after having climbed a ramp you enter the fortress by the eastern gate of Fort St. George then cross the drawbridge before walking under the Clock Tower. The latter opened onto the « middle castle », in which the king's quarters were located. At the extreme west end there was a fortified redoubt, called Fort du Coudray, in one of whose towers Joan of Arc stayed. And yet, because your reconstitution of the castle is imperfect, you may dream in the shade of a section of wall where a chimney hangs in empty space, and imagine poor Charles VIII, hunted and spied upon, suspiciously receiving this young unknown girl who had come to help him get his kingdom back. During the Hundred Years War, Chinon lived its last great hours. Peace was to leave it useless and out of style. Time and the forgetfulness of human beings were to complete the ruin of this now deserted royal domain.

As you come down from the castle the old town invites you for a stroll along Voltaire Street, at the foot of the cliff. A series of old stone or half-timbered houses constitutes a group of exceptional unity. Many houses are surrounded by minuscule courtyards and small gardens hanging from the rock which are overrun by Virginia creeper, ivy and wisteria. A few handsome churches are to be seen as you stroll-through the old quarter : the former church of St. Mexme, now only half its earlier size, is Romanesque ; St. Maurice's owes its fame to its vault of very pure Angevin style and St. Stephen's to its fine flamboyant door.

It is impossible to speak of Chinon without mentioning its nearby forest, whose immensity also hides a few handsome ruins. The abbeys of Turpenay and Pommier Aigre (Sour Apple Tree) are today in ruins, but as you go looking for them you will have a long walk on the path of Louis XI's hunting lodge, Forges de Bonaventure.

Once back at Chinon, before crossing the Vienne and reaching the other bank, you must make a detour to Véron. Situated between the Loire and the Vienne, this flat country of the watershed of both rivers possesses castles that are in the main unknown. Velors, being too close to a tentacular power plant and hidden by a curtain of trees, can hardly be seen from the road. The castle was built in the late fifteenth century and enlarged in the seventeenth century with pavilions and outbuildings. One reaches the main courtyard through a monumental gate. Closing the courtyard, the fifteenth-century living quarters show a white façade dotted with bricks in no particular geometrical pattern as at

Chatigny or Réaux. This local decorative device is used here with great imagination! All the charm of Velors is due to this original decoration and to the luminosity of its façades in the sun. You have only to cross the high-road to find another manor-house, Baronnière, which has been forgotten by everyone.

On the Véron soil the density of late medieval and Renaissance castles and manor-houses is amazing : Destilly, Razilly, Coulaine and Courtinière, whose musical names alone call to mind houses that were agreeable to live in. In spite of its being deserted and defaced, Courtinière has kept a little of its splendor of former days. Built in mid-sixteenth century, it boasts a military apparatus of crenelles and machicolations, made unseemly by the profuse sculptured decorations. This richness is surprising on such a small structure. It is one of the last castles before the junction of the Vienne and the Loire at Candes. Véron, a little tongue of land bounded by the two rivers, ends here. To appreciate the countryside you must climb the steep slopes of the cliff behind the Candes church. From there you can see during the summer low tides sandbanks between which the two rivers try to meet. The fall and spring floods, which inundate this flat country, keep you from seeing this watershed, but give another aspect of it. On the other bank of the Vienne is

Rabelais's country, a moderate and amiable soil, suited to delicate crops. The little valley of the Ligron at Devinière, where Rabelais was born, was the setting of the Picrocholean War, but other places call to mind these imaginary battles: Lerné, Seuilly and La Roche-Clermaut, which were the important places in the world of Rabelais's characters.

Le Coudray-Montpensier castle seems to be a part of this world. From a high hill, its aggressive towers overlook Seuilly and the entire Chinon country-side. You enter this fifteenth century moat-encircled fortress through a gate let into a tall square tower. The stern block of living quarters is flanked by tall buttressed towers which are crowned with merlons. Few castles in Touraine, except for Langeais, still have so defensive an appearance.
Opposite Chinon, the hill on the left bank, which is fairly distant from the river, is covered with forests. On this back-ground of greenery stand out the light-colored façades of La Vauguyon, Plessis-Gerbault and Vaugaudry. The abundance of these little castles, the beauty of the most humble farms as well as the richness of the soil and the mildness of the climate make of the area around Chinon a real land of milk and honey. At some distance from the Vienne, Marçay typifies this architecture of the Chinonais. This fifteenth-century edifice, which was rebuilt and remodelled in the sixteenth century,

unites the vestiges of feudal elegance to the novelties of the country house : the combination of two absolutely different ways of life which gives these houses an original character.

On the banks of the Veude, a small tributary of the Vienne, Le Rivau is one of the castles of the Chinonais that have suffered least from restorations. In spite of the disappearance of the chapel and the razing of some of the living quarters, it still has a great deal of character. The thirteenth-century keep, proudly standing in the southern part, contains the carriage entrance of the drawbridge. The large block of living quarters, facing eastward, is flanked by two cylindrical towers at the corners and a polygonal turret in the center of the façade. To the north, a little square pavilion has a gate topped with a watch turret. In the outbuildings are semi- circular barrel-vaulted stables and in the courtyard a Renaissance fountain with a broad basin.

To the south, toward the lands of the Richelais and their vast horizons, Champigny-on-Veude retains only the memory of its castle. Richelieu, a jealous neighbor, ordered its destruction in the early seventeenth century. In the park, the Sainte-Chapelle fortunately escaped this delirium of destruction. Begun in 1510 and finished in 1548, it is of Gothic conception but its decoration is inspired by Renaissance themes. The entrance is preceded by a peristyle with pilasters and columns supporting the entablature which is ornamented with a frieze. The walls are richly decorated with garlands, medallions and niches containing statues. But the main interest of this seigniorial chapel lies in the magnificent Renaissance stained glass which fills the tall windows with flamboyant color. Not far from there, on a hill, a country lord had built during the reign of Louis XIV an immense château, La Grillière, whose long stone façade is stretched out on a single level and topped by attics where dormer windows alternate with small circular windows. The forepart of the building, topped with a triangular pediment, accentuates the center of the structure and gives it classical majesty which is unexpected in this unpretentious countryside.

The region has been subject to excessive projects. It was a few kilometers from there that Cardinal de Richelieu conceived the project of a new town and a palace. The little town that dozes today in the heart of the Richelais is spread over a rectangle 700 meters long and 500 meters wide (approximately 2333 feet by 1666 feet). It is arranged around the main avenue which serves as the central axis for identical mansions and cross-streets. The château, the work of the architect Lemercier, was demolished during the Restoration. Only a few parts have been spare : the entrance pavilion, the orange greenhouse and the outbuildings which can still be seen in the handsome park.

After Richelieu, we leave Touraine for the Loudunais or region of Loudun, at the border of Poitou. Between Loudun and Mirebeau, three castles still belong to the Vale of the Loire. Roche-du-Maine occupies a traditional site on a bare ridge in the middle of a plain. Surrounded by a now-dry moat, the castle, which was built around 1520, unites feudal defense elements with Renaissance decoration. The latter, of a richness common in the Vale of the Loire, is carried out in fine stone of exceptional quality. Its neighbor, the château of Coussay, situated on the rolling hills of the Mirebelais, was built in the early sixteenth century by an important burger of Touraine who had become a prelate. The decoration, like that at Azay-le-Rideau, is limited to the dormer windows and to the window and door facings and can stand comparison with that of the château on the banks of the Indre. The flexibility of the design and the finesse of relief of the foliage and arabesques give this edifice incomparable grace. At the entrance to the forecourt on the side of the farm buildings, an elegant pavilion contains a fountain where the refinement of the sculpted decoration is inexplicable considering the use to which the building was put. South of Loudun, Oiron, situated in the heart of a vast plain, can be seen from very far away. The château displays the juxtaposition of a Renaissance wing and a large classical pavilion built in the seventeenth century on the site of a former dwelling house. The Renaissance structure, which was begun in 1516, was finished only in 1559. The remaining part opens on the ground floor onto a gallery whose arches are supported by twisted pillars. The latter are topped with niches which formerly contained statues and terra cotta ornaments. The upper floor of this gallery, lighted by broad windows, contains a long room entirely covered with frescoes whose theme is the Trojan War. On the borders of Touraine, this pictorial group, which was directly inspired by the Gallery of Ulysses at Fontainebleau, surprises us by its size and allows us to imagine the luxurious life in the province during the sixteenth century.

VALLÉE DE LA CREUSE
ET DE LA VIENNE
VALLEYS OF THE CREUSE AND THE VIENNE

118. Parc de Champigny-sur-Veude
118. Park of Champigny-on-Veude

119 | 120

119. Château du Rivau
119. Le Rivau Castle

120. Champigny-sur-Veude : vitrail de la chapelle
120. Champigny-on-Veude : stained glass window in the chapel

121. Vue aérienne du château de Chinon
121. Aerial view of Chinon Castle

8

THE LOIR VALEY

The north of the Vale of the Loire is bounded by a single waterway, the Loir, which serves as natural boundary to Anjou, Touraine and the Blesois. It is a different river from the tributaries of the south, whose valleys break the monotony of the plateau. It flows slowly in a wide valley. Its loops and meanders are edged with rows of trees, pollard oaks, willows and young elms, which signal its presence from afar.

The landscape, with is sometimes monotonous in Anjou and in northern Touraine, is not without charm here. In winter, the high waters overflow onto the vast prairie. Over the sleeping countryside then spreads the heavy silence of the flooded plains broken only at times by a bird's cry. Near Vendôme, the relief is more rugged, and the Loir flows around hills, cliffs and promontories. Sometimes rounding a loop or a steep crag, you come upon a mill, a keep or a castle showing its blue-roofed outline.

Near its junction with the Sarthe, the valley, deeper now, was the site of one of the region's most beautiful castles. Le Verger, now in ruins, is known through many seventeenth century drawings which enable us to imagine the magnificence of the residence. Built in the fate fifteenth century by Pierre de Rohan, it bore some ressemblance to an Angevin castle already-mentioned, Plessis-Bourré. The latter exercised a definite influence on Le Verger, particularly in the disposition of the living quarters between two low wings.

Following the valley in the direction of Durtal, we find the Loir full of charm. On its banks ends the forest of Chambiers, one of the most beautiful and largest in Anjou. Durtal, built in the sixteenth century by a companion of Francis I, is a formidable edifice which rises from a promontory above the river. Between Durtal and Baugé, the more pleasant Gastines is now freed of the modern structures that crushed it and appears graceful and charming. Built under Henry II, it is a rustic manor-house whose beauty resides mainly in the fine proportions of its buildings of unequalheights. Baugé, although it is far from the Loir, occupies a particular position in the heart of the Angevin forests. In the center of an agreeable town stands the castle built by Yolanda of Aragon on the site of an older fortress. Remodelled later by her son René of Anjou, it is in no way a sumptuous edifice. It is an unostentatious gentleman's home, whose elegant flamboyant decoration is at its most splendid in the great staircase. The town retains a few vestiges of this royal past: a curious church surmounted by a spiral steeple and a hospital with its seventeenth century pharmacy.

On the outskirts, we discover handsome churches, like the one at Pouligné, which is decorated with frescoes, and the one at Bocé where Romanesque sculpture ennobles the façade. At Mouliherne, the twelfth-century church is covered with one of the first Angevin vaults. Near La Flèche, the well-named village, Saint-Germain-du-Val-Perché (St. Germain of the Hanging Valley), is worth a visit because of its location overlooking the Loir Valley as far as Lude.
Lude, a fortress built by the Daillon family, commanded the access to the Loir during the Hundred Years War. Its reconstruction was undertaken in

the late fifteenth century but was finished only at the end of the following century. The castle is composed of four wings with a tower at each corner, forming a square inner courtyard. The history of the construction is too complex to be summarized and you will be more sensitive here to the setting of greenery than to architectural matters. The gardens and terraces that slope down to the Loir surround the castle in a jewel box of water and vegetation. The loops of the river encircle the building, illuminating it with dancing light.

Before reaching Château-du-Loir, the Loir swallows up an infinity of streams which take their source in northern Touraine. The Maulne, the Escotais, the Nais and the Dême have small valleys which often hold the surprise of a château, a picturesque village or a church. On the Maulne, Marcilly is totally forgotten, situated as it is at the northernmost point of Touraine ; it was built during the first years of the seventeenth century. The majestic appearance of the structure and its regular plan announce the coming of the classical period. To the south, near Château-la-Vallière, a forest hides the ruins of a fortress. Vaujours, once called Val Joyeux, stands in the hollow of a deep, narrow wooded valley. The beauty of the site is in keeping with the fanciful sight of cracked tower watts and razed perimeter watts surrounded by marshes.

At the source of the Fare, La Motte-Sonzay, a solid structure with corner-towers, would call to mind some sudden attack of the Hundred Years War if its façade had not been remodelled in the Renaissance style. In the surrounding countryside, a country seat which charms us by the sound of its name, Naudésir, rises above the Valley of the Escotais. The main living quarters have remained unchanged since their construction in the late sixteenth Century. Surrounded by a broad moat, it is topped by a steep roof with beautiful dormer windows with double openings. The regular façade with pilaster-framed, mullioned windows let into it makes us think of moderation and harmony.

The neighboring château of Roche-Racan belonged, as its name indicates, to the poet Racan who had it rebuilt in the seventeenth Century. It is integrated into a splendid landscape of water and greenery, an association native to Touraine, as we know.

The course of the Long, a vagabond-stream, leads us to our last stop in northern Touraine, the village of Bueil. It has two very interesting churches : the parish church of St Peter of the Bonds and the collegiate church, St. Michael's. The former, begun in 1480 and consecrated in 1512, is richly decorated in a style typical of the early Renaissance. In the nave, sixteenth-century baptismal fonts are composed of stone basins topped with elaborate-ly carved wooden lids. The latter church was founded in the fate fourteenth century and has a sixteenth-century crypt which before the French Revolution contained recumbent statues on the tombs of the Bueil family.

After this short incursion into Touraine, we rejoin the Loir at La Chartre where it divides into several arms and encloses the town. Not far from there is Poncé, which owes its fame to a magnificent Renaissance staircase whose straight flights are covered with coffered vaulting. The latter are decorated with lively, fanciful motifs : coats-of-arms, cupids and salamanders alternate with masks, medallions, mascarons and a profusion of plant elements. Numbering 136 and all different, they constitute this manor-house's only luxury. Opposite the château the terraces overlooking the Loir are planted with a curions labyrinth of yoke-elms arranged around a hundred-year-old plane tree. The Romanesque village church is decorated with frescoes like most Loir Valley churches. After Poncé the landscape broadens and the wider horizon permits us to see the first curves of the Vendômois. Between Poncé and Vendôme, other châteaux, fortresses and churches make each village an interesting place.

La Possonière manor-house was the cradle of the Ronsard family. The rather modest living quarters, dating from the early sixteenth Century, are enriched by a door a dormer window of great refinement. Inside is a highly decorated Renaissance chimney, one of the best preserved of the Loire Valley. The courtyard is bounded on the east by a rocky mass housing seven caves whose entrances were decorated in the sixteenth century with mottoes and sayings engraved on lintels. The poet's parents were cultivated people, art lovers and humanists. The house descended to Ronsard's brother but the poet stayed there frequently ; he sang in many poems of this Loir Valley.

From La Possonière to Vendôme it is called the « valley of frescoes » because of the many Romanesque churches decorated with murals. Saint-Jacques-des-Guérets is the best-known one because of the variety of painted scenes there and the beauty of the colors. The coppery tones are reminiscent of miniatures and are closer to Gothic painting than to the Romanesque shades seen in the region. Troo, a curious troglodyte village, has a Romanesque chapel decorated with frescoes. It is overshadowed by its neighbor, Saint-Gilles-de-Montoire. Situated in the suburb of Saint-Oustrille this private chapel is now half in ruins. The frescoes covering its walls are considered the most beautiful Romanesque paintings of the valley. The free-flowing movement and the lightness of the colors

make them an exceptional ensemble. Montoire is built on a hill at the summit of which stands a ruined keep and it is encircled by a loop of the Loir. Near the town at the place called Bois-Freslon, a fortified manor-house stands on a wooded hill. Further away, Courtanvaux castle has an agreeable name that is not belied by the structure itself. It surprises us by thedazzling whiteness of its façades which we discover beyond a monumental entrance flanked by towers. The region is well provided with fortresses and keeps! Taking the direction of Lavardin, we see from afar the impressive square tower called the « Shoulder ». Gigantic and perched on a great rock, these ruins look like fragments of enormous bones. The parish church presents a complete panorama of mural painting of the twelfth of the fifteenth Century.

Near Vendôme the Loir's loops increase in number. At Gué-du-Loir it wraters Bonaventure manor-house, now only a modest farm which, like the song, is forgotten. Vendôme was the cradle of the powerful counts of the same name, one of France's greatest feudal families until the sixteenth century. We enter the town by St. George's gate, which is flanked by two big towers dating from the fourteenth century, and whose opening was widened in the last century to permit the passage of a national highway. Handsome churches in a large park, the castle ruins and a few dwelling houses maintain the ancient character of this town. The present Ronsard Lycée, a college for Oratorian fathers founded in the seventeenth century by César de Vendôme, is situated in a gardon washed by the Loir. In town, bridges and foot-bridges span the river which is ramified into several branches.

The town's jewel is Trinity church, which was built tram the fourteenth to the sixteenth century. It is surmounted by a very tall bell-tower whose proportions symbolize formal perfection. The choir and the front façade are masterpieces of flamboyant Gothic art. Inside, magnificient stained glass enlivens the tall windows and the splendid rose window in the entrance. The stone screen that separates the choir from the ambulatory and the fountain from the nave is from the Renaissance period.

Outside of Vendôme the Loir encircles hills and promontories, speckled with villages dug into the rock. Although the valley looks very much the same, the surrounding countryside changes little by little. Vast stretches of treeless land foretell the wheatfields of Beauce. The light is more mineral-like and the wind, unhampered by any grove of trees, sometimes swells the waves of grain.

In this land of clay where stone is rare, the buildings are of a different color: pink brick has replaced white tufa. Near Vendôme, Vievy-le-Rayé,

Renay, Glatigny and Saint-Agil, with its refined Renaissance decoration, are made of brick. Modest as it is in appearance, this material gives the buildings a melancholy touch as at Plessis-Saint-Amand. This Louis XIII château, with its brick walls and stone ties, is a place that calls to mine a poetic reminiscence, a « fancy » of Gérard de Nerval :

« Then a brick château with stone
*   corners*
With windowglass stained in reddish
*   colors,*
Girded by great parks with a river...»

The end of the poem is very sad and we can't leave the laughing Loir Valley on such a disenchanted note.

Chateaudun, in spite of its northerly situation, should, because of its castle, be associated with the art of the Loire. The town occupies a strategic situation on a steep rock. Built by Dunois in the fifteenth century, the imposing fortress overlooks the valley.

The thick walls which grip the rocksolidly and are shored up by buttresses, have nothing of the Loire's gentleness. We will understand the relationship only after having entered the courtyard : a delightful flamboyant chapel leans against the ancien keep while ancient L-shaped living quarters close trie perimeter wall. Built in the fifteenth century, these living quarters are flanked by elegant watchtowers and a polygonal turret and have broad windows with prismatic mullioned windows. These features give a certain finesse to the building, but they are overshadowed by the wonder of the castle : a monumental staircase which joins the two wings of the living quarters and opens on each floor onto a double loggia with very fine flamboyant decoration.

All during this outing, I have wanted to tell of a unique artistic heritage. My modest purpose was to avoid limiting the Vale of the Loire to this « Renaissance land », famous because of several great châteaux that one visits traditionally. This goal will have been reached if I awake the reader's curiosity as I guide him outside the beaten paths.

9

THE GREAT CHÂTEAUX
OF THE LOIRE

AMBOISE

Two large towers, elegant royal living quarters, the very charming St. Hubert's chapel, oratory of queens, and a terrace overlooking the Loire - this is Amboise castle, one of the greatest. Its rebirth dates from the lime of Charles VIII, and Philippe de Commines tells us that the artists in charge of the gardens and buildings came from Naples. Among them was Il Boccador. The young king wanted this to be his « earthly paradise ». He met his death here in 1498 after hitting his head against the lintel of a door.

Francis I used the castle for lavish parties, which may have been attended by Leonardo da Vinci, the king's friend, who lived at Clos Lucé.

A curtain falls on joy, death returns with the Amboise Conspiracy in 1560. La Renaudie's Protestants are hanged from the balconies and thrown into the Loire.

Under Louis XIV, Amboise was a prison « frequented » by Fouquet and Lauzun. During the Empire it was hardly better, Roger Ducos, a former member of the Directory, being the owner.

Amboise then returned to the House of France, a branch of the Orleans family, which recently donated it to the St. Louis Foundation, whose patron the Count of Paris is.

Between 1848 and 1853 Emir Abd El-Kader, who was exiled at Amboise, was an occupant of the castle. He lived in the king's quarters, including the Hall of the Estates.

At Clos Lucé (fifteenth century), a few steps away, we can call to mind the great da Vinci; the well-preserved house is a museum devoted to his memory.

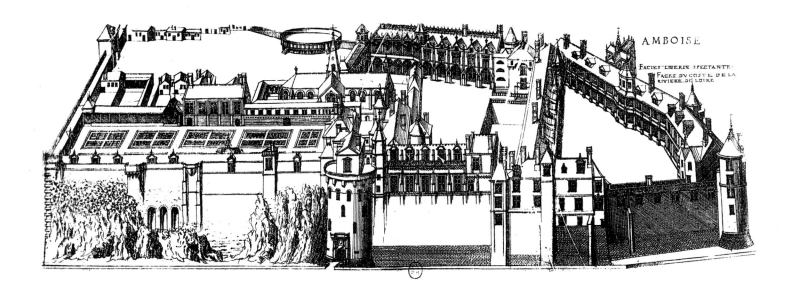

AZAY-LE-RIDEAU

It is the most characteristic of the châteaux of the Loire even though it is the Indre that feeds its moat. It was built from 1518 to 1529 for Gilles Berthelot, the king's treasurer.

After the financier Semblançay was hanged at Montfaucon, Berthelot, who was compromised in the affair, became frightened, lied and abandoned Azay to Francis I. We are still profiting from the « gift ». Azay is a very pleasant and very human size. It unites the graces of the Renaissance and the rigidity of the Middle Ages : lace on a healthy skin. And the moat is placed exactly at the place where, in autumn, the leaves rail, for, of course, Azay is set among trees and its « curtain » is green or reddish-brown, according to the season.

Mullioned windows, pilasters, dormer windows and sculpted pinnacles, little columns, niches and friezes, gables and machicolations (which could almost be from an operetta) are adorned with ermines and salamanders. The façades are splendid and the towers well placed. Harmony reigns over Azay where nothing is very surprising except the perfect success of the undertaking.

In 1870 while Francis Charles of Prussia was staying there, a chandelier fell on a table. It was feared that this was an assassination attempt and Azay barely escaped being destroyed.

One must visit it and climb the great staircase situated behind the large gable.

There is a museum of the Renaissance here; it is quite at home.

CHAMBORD

Immense and yet light, singular, legendary Chambord on the Cosson is in the middle of a 5000 hectare (12,500 acre) park enclosed by thirty- two kilometers (twenty-two miles) of walls. Francis I had the château built so that he could hunt there. For twelve years, 1800 workers labored on it. In 1539 when Emperor Charles V came to visit, it was not completed, but the double spiral stair-case had already been built. It is well-known that it permits persans going up and down to see each other through openings without meeting. Bell-turrets, dormer windows, lantern-turrets and chimneys on the roofs oppose their extraordinary stone forest to the real forest nearby in the park. Under Henry II the chapel was built. We shall skip other kings, even Henry IV, to find Chambord under Louis XIII in the hands of Gaston d'Orléans. But it was in 1660 under Louis XIV that Mansart did considerable remodelling to lodge the king's retinue, which allowed Molière to play Monsieur de Pourceaugnac and Le Bourgeois Gentilhomme for the first time before the court. Stanislas Leszczynski, Louis XV's father-in-law, lived here long enough to have the moat filled, which was a mistake. Then came Field Marshal de Saxe, the victor at Fontenoy, who lodged two cavalry regiments composed of Wallachians, Tartars, Martinicans and a terrified actress named Favart.

During the Empire, Field Marshal Berthier made Chambord the « Principality of Wagram », a very curious thing to do, to say the toast. Later a national subscription saved Chambord and it was given to the Duke of Bordeaux in spite of Paul Louis Courier's protests. Today Chambord belongs to the State, which bought it for 11,000,000 francs in 1932 from the heirs of the Count of Chambord.

CHEVERNY

In this land of invention that the Loire countryis, Cheverny's classicism is surprising but agreeably so. The unfinished southern façade has niches for busts. The completed northern façade would be austere if it were not for the handsome store bridge spanning the moat. This residence was completed in 1634 by Henry Hurault, Count of Cheverny and son of a chancellor of Henry II and Henry IV. The de Vibraye family, another branch of the Chevernys, are the present owners. The park is beautiful with its woods and ornamental ; lakes, but one must see the inside of the castle,which is remarkably rich.

Decoration, beams, elaborate chimneys, famous paintings, tapestries, drawing rooms and guardrooms, gallery and king's chamber, everything here is an art lesson.

And you may be fortunate enough to see a stag hunt when you visit Cheverny.

VALLÉE DU LOIR
VALLEY OF THE LOIR

124. Vendôme : clé historiée d'une voûte du transept de la Trinité
124. Vendôme : bell-tower of the former abbey of the Trinity

128. Entrée de la commanderie d'Arville
128. Entrance of the Commandery of Arville

129. Ruines du château de Lavardin
129. Ruins of Lavardin Castle

130 | 131

130. *Château du Lude : Grand salon*
130. *Château of Le Lude : Great drawing room*

131. *Château du Lude : cabinet des peintures*
131. *Château of Le Lude : painting's room*

THE GREAT CHÂTEAUX
OF THE LOIRE

BLOIS

Sitting at the top of the city, the château is a rich lesson in architecture and history combined.

A lesson in architecture because after Charles d'Orléans, ex-prisoner of the English, a prince-poet who held court at Blois from 1440 to 1464 (he entertained François Villon, among others), Louis XII, his son, had the eastern façade built and placed an equestrian statue of himself there. In architecture again because Francis I, on the basis of Denis Sourdeau's plans, built the façade of the Loggias and the famous staircase, a Renaissance jewel. In architecture again because we owe to Gaston d'Orléans the seventeenth century living quarters that were designed by Mansart.

A lesson in history because Blois was the theater of great events : the betrothal of the future Henry IV (1572), the assassination of the Duke of Guise (1588) in Henry III's apartment (Francis I wing) and the Estates General (1576 and 1588).

Deserted for a Century, in 1788 the castle became a caserne. Its restoration was begun in 1845.

Inside and outside, a long visit is a must.

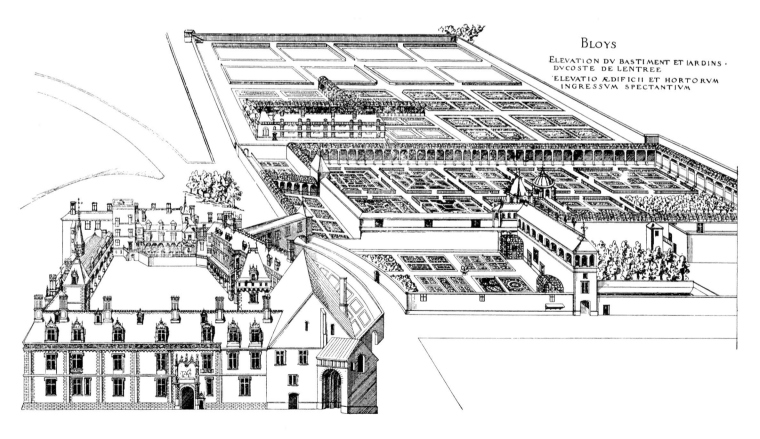

BLOYS
ELEVATION DV BASTIMENT ET IARDINS·
DVCOSTE DE LENTREE
ELEVATIO ÆDIFICII ET HORTORVM
INGRESSVM SPECTANTIVM

CHAUMONT

Five towers, one of which is square. There would have been seven if one of the occupants had not wanted to have an opening onto the Loire and had the terrace built. Chaumont belonged to the Amboise family before Catherine de' Medici. It was here that the celebrated queen worked with the astrologer Ruggieri to know what the future held in store for her. Prudent and perhaps superstitious, Catherine was also vindictive. Diane of Poitiers having stolen her husband, soon after the death of Henri II Catherine forced her rival to give her Chenonceau and in turn gave Chaumont to Diane.

It was not before the eighteenth century that Chaumont was turned into a pottery under the direction of the Italian, Nini, a famous ceramist and engraver on glass, and thus came back to life.

Lovers of the medieval style will get their fill at Chaumont of towers and a drawbridge. Those who prefer the Renaissance will find a handsome well and, inside, a chapel, paneling and period floor tiles. Others can dream above the Loire which Chaumont dominates with its solid mass.

CHENONCEAU

A château-bridge on the calm Cher, but what a bridge, what a château and what gardons around them! In February, 1513, financier-baron Bohier bought the property from the Marques family and together with his wife, Clatherine Briçonnet, had the château built.

Diane of Poitiers, Henry II's mistress, had the bridge built, and her rival, Catherine de' Medici, the gallery over it.

When to these three lady-builders you have added the melancholy Louise of Lorraine, Henry III's widow, the inconsolable « queen in white », you will have reached the summit of womanhood in action and in prayer.

Just before the Revolution came Madame Dupin whose son was tutored by Jean-Jacques Rousseau, who spoke in glowing terms of this happy time in his Confession.

In 1864, a Madame Pelouze bought the château and made its renovation her life's work.

If one had to give a prize for pomp to one of these ladies, it would go to Catherine de' Medici who gave magnificent parties in the days before Henry III's rustic banquet, which cost 100,000 pounds. Not long before, the Bohiers had bought the property of Chenonceau for 12,000 pounds.

CHINON

Three ruined fortresses crown the rocky spur of Chinon above the Vienne. Philip Augustus, king of France, took them away from Henry II and Richard the Lion-hearted. Charles VII, « King of Bourges », was living in the central castle when he received in the great hall a young peasant girl of eighteen, Joan of Arc, who had to discover him, somewhat disguised, among three hundred persons. Born of an inconstant mother, the dauphin doubted that he was the king's son. Joan reassured him and the war to free France began (1429).

Chinon kept the court until the middle of the fifteenth century and it was here that the Papal Legate, Caesar Borgia, came to deliver Louis XII from his first wife who was outrageously humpbacked but daughter of Louis XI. That allowed the gaffant king to marry later Charles VII's widow, that Anne who brought Britanny to France. Walking down a footpath, we can dream in these castles. The last illustrious owner was Cardinal de Richelieu.

But you must alse go down into Old Chinon, which is all the more worth the trouble since one can brighten up the outing with a good red wine and the no less savory memory of Rabelais who spent his childhood at La Devinière, several miles away.

LOCHES

We are in the Middle Ages and the ghost of Agnes Sorel, who was the favorite of Charles VII, hardly blurs the armor of Richard the Lion-hearted and Philip Augustus, who fought over this fortress. The keep is a handsome structure but the Martelet will make you shudder because of its dungeons (Loches was used as a prison), in particular that of Ludovico il Moro, Duke of Milan, who was imprisoned there for eight years and died of light the day he was freed, that of the rebellious Bishops of Le Puy and Autun and that of the Count of Saint-Vallier, Diane of Poitier's father, who learned of his pardon on the gallows. In the round tower, La Ballue who had been made cardinal by Louis XI but had betrayed him to Charles the Bold, was confined in a very tight cage known as a « little girl ». St. Ursus's church with its four bell-towers of Romanesque style enables us to escape from this depravity.

Loches is a town as much as a castle. You should walk inside the medieval walls from the gates to the king's quarters while dreaming of an imaginary meeting with Thierry la Fronde or Robin Hood.

VALENÇAY

Financiers, Farmers General, John Law and Talleyrand were the successive owners ; this remarkable castle was very lucky. The colossal and yet elegant keep at the outrance and the roofs and domed towers strike a happy medium between the Renaissance and classical styles. The three courtyards and the apartments are very large. One visits only part of the latter.

It is well-known that Napoleon had Talleyrand purchase Valençay so that he could entertain statesmen here. The most illustrious was King Ferdinand VII of Spain, who was courteously treated while he was a prisoner here from 1808 to 1814. The former Bishop of Autun lavished care on this residence, which was worthy of his family. He embellished the castle and added about 20,000 hectares (50,000 acres) to it. From this period there still romain drawing rooms and handsome furniture which were used for receptions, some of which were magnificent.

The Prince's chamber has been reconstituted and historical souvenirs enable us to evoke this relatively faithful servant of many different regimes. In the gardons and on the balustrades magnificently plumed peacocks parade among other birds and animals of varions sorts : Valençay is highly colored in every detail.

VILLANDRY

A very beautiful French-style garden « embroidered » with box-trees and yews, where the borders represent the different forms of love, captures our attention so thoroughly that we almost forget the kitchen garden and the water garden with its beautiful mirror-like sheet of water.

This masterpiece, the only one of its kind in France, is due to Dr. Carvallo who, around 1906, decided to reconstruct the former sixteenth-century gardens, which had been created by Gaillon. The owner had to plow up the English garden, clear the moat, reconstruct the terraces and reconnect the circuits of water pipes. Considering the extent and complexity of the work, this was admirably done. The water, plant geometry and sculpted stone have benefitted more from it than nature, no doubt.

The château is less deserving of admiration because it has been remodelled several times.

Villandry houses a museum of considerable interest (Goya, Herrera, Zurbaran and others).

Jean Le Breton, in the sixteenth century, and, more recently, the Castellanes and even Napoleon and his brother Joseph lived here.

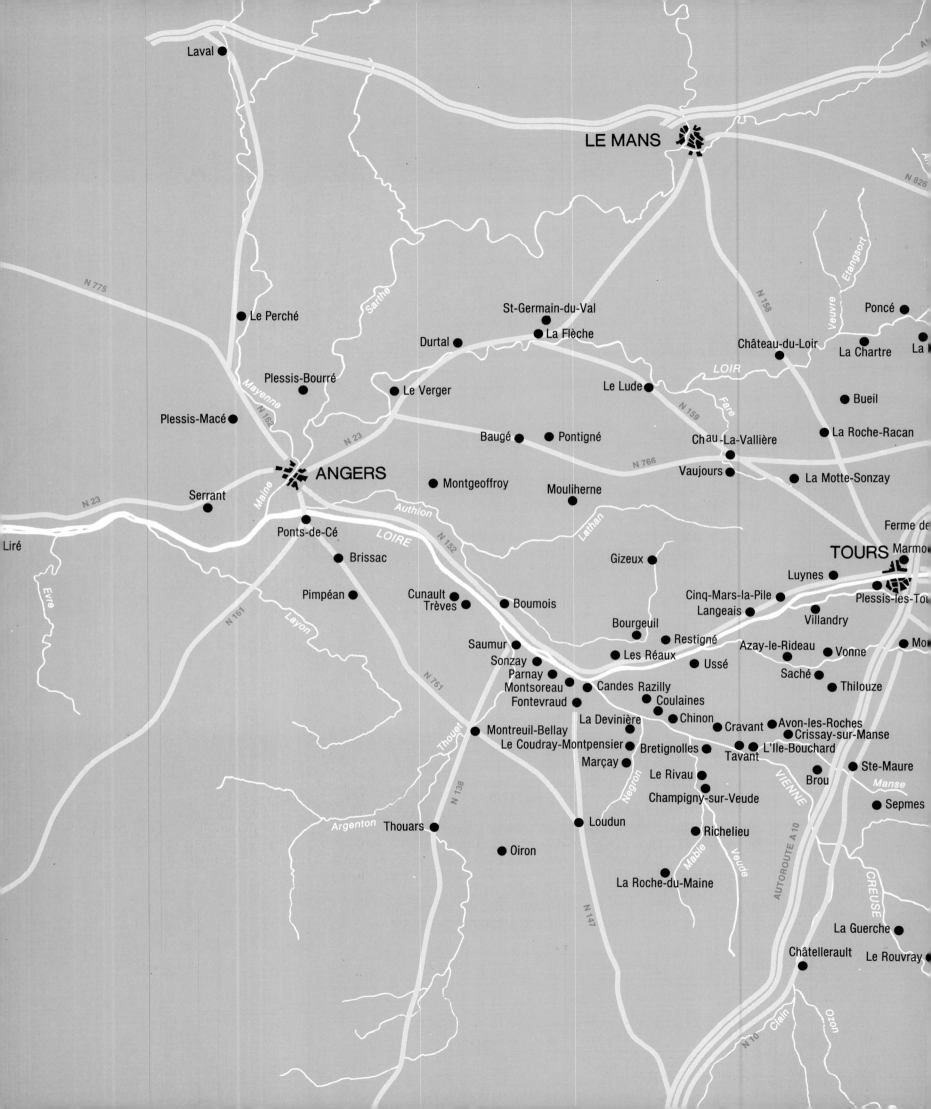

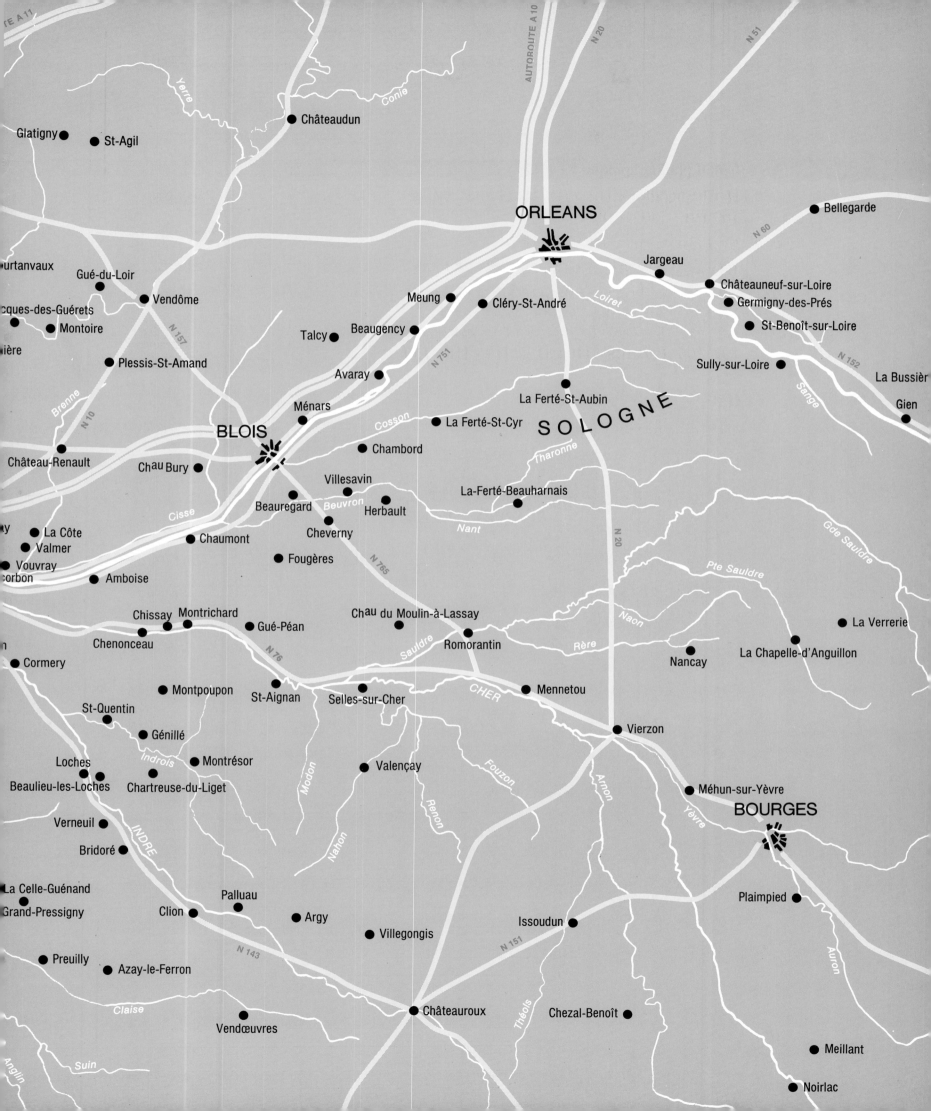

LES CHÂTEAUX DE LA LOIRE
a été réalisé
par les Éditions Hermé à Paris

Collection L'ALBUM
dirigée par Michel Laugel

Texte de Annie Cospérec

Édition Bénédicte Baussan

Maquette de Michel Labarthe

Suivi technique CPE

Papier semi-mat 170 g.
des papeteries Garda

Reliure SIRC

Diffusion Hermé

Achevé d'imprimer le 30 mars 1997
pour le compte des Éditions Hermé à Paris
© 1997 by Éditions Hermé - Paris (France)
Imprimé en France
ISBN .2-86665-220-7 (Édition anglaise)